The Cake & Cookie Closet

ALL DOLLED UP IN SUGAR

DEBRA J. MOSELY

AuthorHouse™
1663 Liberty Drive
Bloomington, IN 47403
www.authorhouse.com
Phone: 1-800-839-8640

First published by AuthorHouse 3/23/2010

ISBN: 978-1-4389-7133-9 (sc)

Library of Congress Control Number: 2009911533

Printed in the United States of America
Bloomington, Indiana

This book is printed on acid-free paper.

authorHOUSE®

Contents

Acknowledgements.. ii

Introduction...Come into my Cake & Cookie Closet........................... iii

Chapter 1
    Dresses 1

Chapter 2
    Shoes & Boots 22

    Boot Cookies 29

Chapter 3
    Hats 30

Chapter 4
    Pants 36

Chapter 5
    Purses 39

Chapter 6
    Accessories 45

Chapter 7
    What's In Your Closet? Important Techniques 49

Chapter 8
    Tools and Equipment 51

Chapter 9
    Storing and Transporting Your Cakes and Cookies 52

Chapter 10
    Gift and Party Ideas 53

Chapter 11
    My Favorite Recipes 54

Chapter 12
    Suppliers/Favorite Websites 63

Index 64

About the Author & Photographer..65

Chapter 13
    Templates 67

Acknowledgements

My amazing mother, Jannie Lee Mosely, has always inspired me with her beauty and strength, and I thank God for her. My father, Elliott Mosely, is creative and loves working on cars. My brothers Gregory and Glen were the first to be guinea pigs for my creations, and I am happy they still eagerly try out new creations. I love them dearly. My nephews Tyrell Mitchell, Gregory Mosley, Jr., Chase Fleming Williams, and Jamar Mitchell fill my heart with joy and keep me active. They are always giving me reasons to try something new.

I'm blessed to be surrounded by a lot of loving relatives. My aunts are beautiful women, and each talented in their own right - Annice Jones, Clarice Burney, Gayzell Mosely, Rosie Abram, Estella Robinson, Revil Mosely, Odessia Birks, Annie Witherspoon, Susie Witherspoon, Patricia Brown, Lucy Witherspoon, Maggie Lee Williams, and Annie Daniels. They have shared their love and wisdom with me over the years, and I enjoy their company. My uncles are strong men with gentle hearts - Wiley Jones, Sr., James Witherspoon, Wilbert Witherspoon, Sam Birks, Sr., Jimmy Burney, Kenny Fells, Otis Abram, Gil Williams, and Walter Robinson. I thank each one and am grateful for all of our talks over the years. My godmother, Leanna Watts, is an angel sent by God to watch over me, and I'll love you always. I am thankful also to some of my loving and very talented cousins - Carolyn Best, Heather Mosely, Charleta Mosely Harvey, Gloria Abram, Wiley Jones, Jr., Louise Williams, Stephanie and Ronnie Mosely, Karen Mosley Smith, Linda Mosley, Matthew Jones, DeWayne Jones, Walter Robinson, Jr., Larry Witherspoon, and Cynthia Pagan.

Dear friends are one of life's greatest joys, and I am honored to share my life with some incredibly talented and loving people. Carolyn Fleming Williams and Tony Williams are my special VIPs, and I am an honorary auntie for their son Chase. Margaret Davis is a special VIP, and I thank God for her wisdom and style. To my other VIPs – Wanda Burks, Bonnie Smith, Monique Colbert, Trudie & Tiffany Mitchell, Geveria Scott, Purcell, Jonathan & Preston Johnson, Tartanitia Sims, Josie Pollard, Edith Brown, Janice Brown, Alyssa & David Steinberger, Joanne Fredette & her family, Ingrid Stevenson, Milt Lawler, Diane Foster, Karen & Brenda Hawk, Lois Williams, Tom & Kay Vakerics, Meredith, Caroline & Bennett Ehler, Geraldine & Jim Williams, Mamie Fleming, Rita Ellison, TK Floyd & Benjamin Walton, Jeanne Reeves, Lorna Coleman, Donna Williams, Paul Sicari, Sandra Bryan-Grier, Katrina Clark, Mamie Holmes, James & Gwen Ferguson, Kaysia Earley, Karen Schoenian, Ray Jacobsen, Jennifer Westbrook, Alison Levin, Michael Nadel, Hillary Webber, Eric Conn, Meredith Caskey Parker, Salena Hickman, Dolly Fotta, Sophia Smith, Brenda Kittay, Andrea Hamilton, Sheila Ingram, Sheila Hawkins Johnson & Rick Johnson, LaNita Talley-Black & Quentin Black, Joyce Brown, E. Ann Jones, Angela Kupenda, Matt & Kim Leland, Tia Davis, Benny Hogan, Karen & Hazel Whitby, Ken Russell, Hazariha Hogan, Judy Blanchard, April Tabor, Kim, Ashley and AJ Scott, Steve Ryan, Dorene Tabaka, Patty Brown, Irene Robles, David Crump, Dawn Moss, Gloria Barnes, Ellen Minchilli, Shawnee Buckner, Trina Johnson, Richard Rogers, Richard Sloane, Francine Hochberg-Giuffrida, Aleice Goodwin, Carla Hine, Brian Benko, Jacqueline Browder-Chaffee, Laura Capotosto, Clint Carpenter, Joanna & Phil Kerpen, Paula Enstice, Kelly Falls, Amy Granger, Will Hansen, Justin Holmes, Emre Ilter, Kendra Kinnaird, Stefan Meisner, Jeff Mikoni, Erika Pont, Rahul Rao, Jennifer Ritter, Josh Rogaczewski, Erik Baptist, Peter Tolsdorf, Paul Thompson, Bobby Burchfield, David Rogers, Marilyn Washington, Michele Johnson, Marcella Stafford, Agnes Gaskin, Richelle Ifill, Corliss Jackson, Charnene Freeny, Steve Littlewood, Pamela Mantis, Darryl Sedgewick, Phyllis Spinks, Gerard Cooper, Debra Southerland, Karen Gallagher, Tracy Rice, Tim Waters, Roy Austin, Ja'Don Isaac, Crystal Hinton, Debora Inawati, Angela Orsini, Angela Newsome, Edith Lillie, Jacqueline Reid-Johnson, Bertha Chase, Andre, Janet & Matthew Sergeon, Jeff Coles, Darrile Walker, Rochelle Dunbar, Jay George, Denise Bolds, Bunni Abernathy, George & Cheryl Bowman, Lisa Ashe, Joyce Dandrea, Tim & Emily Scott, and Helen and Vanessa Alford, and Sandra Mallut at Amoretti for her amazing recipe contribution – thank you for allowing me to share my talents with you and your family.

Last but certainly not least, a very special thank you goes out to Sharon Stewart and Alan Tetreault for naming this book. I wanted a name that fit the designs contained inside, and Sharon and Alan quickly responded.

To people who have inspired my life - Oprah Winfrey, Suze Orman, Cathy Hughes, President Barack Obama & First Lady Michelle Obama, Joel & Victoria Osteen, Toba Garrett, Colette Peters, Roland & Marsha Winbeckler, Sylvia Weinstock, Bronwyn Webber, Norman Davis, Buddy Valastro, Duff Goldman and the entire crew at Charm City Cakes, Ron-Ben Israel, Jennifer Dontz, Diane Shavkin, Earlene Moore, Debbie Brown, Warren Brown, Fran Wheat, Sallee McCarthy, owner of Fran's Cake & Candy shop in Fairfax, Virginia, Barbara Kelly, Dennis Stanley, owner of Chantel's Bakery, Sterling, Virginia, Jules Dowler Shepard, and Lindy Smith -- thank you.

Thank you to Lynne Giovani Geers, Teri Watkins and Katina Gillis for assistance regarding photography in this book, and Richard Alternity Greene for illustrating the templates.

Introduction...Come into my Cake & Cookie Closet

I have loved sweets since I was a child spending hot summers in Alabama. My grandmother, Martha Clark Mosely, owned a small grocery store next door to her house, and I enjoyed being able to eat whatever sweets I wanted, whenever I wanted. I would follow my grandmother around the house eagerly waiting for her to go into the kitchen to bake. She made some of the best cakes, cooked chocolate icing, biscuits and blackberry cobbler I have ever tasted.

My grandmother's great tasting desserts were plain to look at, and I thought they should look as good as they tasted. She would laugh when I said something about the way they looked. She thought it was more important for them to taste good. When I started baking cakes, I focused on making them look and taste good. That led me to discover the Wilton Yearbook and many other cake decorating books. Later when I heard through one of my cake clubs that one of my favorite cake decorating book authors, Roland and Marsha Winbeckler, were coming to Maryland to teach a Professional Cake Decorating class, I quickly signed up. It was a great class, and I learned a lot from both of them. Colette Peters is an amazing cake designer, and I was star struck when I got the opportunity to meet her and take her gum paste class. I was more fascinated with talking to her and looking at all of the stuff in her shop than learning the actual gum paste designs. It was a great class, and I know that I will take another with her soon.

Celebrations are a way of life, and a large part of my life. We celebrate each of life's special moments – a child's first birthday, an engagement, a new baby, weddings, retirements, milestone birthdays, a new house or job – are all good reasons to have a great dessert. My family and friends have allowed me to test out new designs and desserts with them over the years, and I love making their favorites.

I have learned that baking is a journey. When you do what you're passionate about and share it with others, it brings you immeasurable joy and makes your desserts even more special to others. So, after family members and friends kept saying that I should sell my creations, I decided it was time to come "out of the closet" to share these designs with you.

HOW TO USE THIS BOOK

Get ready to be creative! Each chapter features cakes and cookies that will inspire you to create and allow you to get multiple uses out of your cake decorating tools. There are numerous ways you can decorate doll cakes, mini hats and various cookies. Fondant or buttercream dresses can be designed to match a person's actual dress or one they wish they had but could not find. Shoes, purses, hats, pants and belts can be made numerous ways, depending on what tool you use. Lace can be used to imprint fondant or buttercream that has crusted. Practice with various kitchen tools and create new embellishment designs on fondant.

I recommend that you flip through the book first to look at the designs and then read Chapter 7 to see all of the techniques I want you to practice to make it easy for you to make the designs. Some of you will be able to look at the picture and know what to do, and others will need to see the technique. I will be posting ideas and new techniques on my Facebook fan page. Keep up with classes and other information on my website – www.thecakeandcookiecloset. com or on Twitter – www.twitter.com/ckecookiecloset.

Come with me into the closet. I hope that you have as much fun creating these designs for your family and friends as I had working on this book.

Debra

Chapter 1
DRESSES

I love designing doll cakes. Since the dress can be designed many different ways, I have never made the same design twice. That makes each doll cake as unique as its recipient. Doll cakes make the perfect centerpiece dessert for bridal showers, milestone birthdays, retirement parties, women's luncheons, or any other time you want to celebrate a special woman or women. Just make sure you have another dessert handy in case they don't want to cut the cake.

BASIC DOLL CAKE INSTRUCTIONS

You Will Need:

Doll cake baked in Wilton Wonder Mold cake pan
1/2 recipe buttercream frosting (if covering with fondant, for buttercream
    dresses use full recipe)
2 lbs fondant
Wilton Doll Pick
(3) 10" cake board each turned with the lines in opposite directions and
    covered in Fanci Foil wrap or a beautiful cake plate

INSTRUCTIONS:

1. Bake your cake recipe in a Wonder Mold cake pan that has been greased and floured. Let cool in pan for 10 minutes, and then invert cake to release from pan, remove center core from pan and then place cake back in pan until completely cool. I do this because the cake has an uneven bottom and if it's removed from the pan to cool, sometimes it will split down the center.

2. Trim the crown off the cake, and cut three even layers.

3. Put frosting between each layer. If you choose to add a filling, place a dam of frosting around the edge of the cake to hold the filling inside the cake.

4. Apply a layer of frosting to the entire cake. Decorate as desired if you're making a buttercream doll design. Otherwise, place in the refrigerator so that the frosting can set before covering it with fondant.

5. When you remove the chilled cake from the refrigerator, take a paper towel and smooth the frosting. It is important to have a smooth surface for your fondant.

6. Roll out the fondant 1/4 inch thick. If you want to use an impression mat, use it now before you cut out the circle. Use even pressure all across the mat so your design will be even with no gaps. Use an 18" cake board as a template and cut out the fondant with a pizza cutter. Then take your finger and smooth the edges of the fondant down. This is your hem, and it should be smooth.

7. Take the same 18" cake circle and slide your fondant on it. Evenly center your fondant over the doll cake base. Once your fondant is on the cake, the bottom of the skirt will go into gentle curves. Use your fingers or a wooden dowel stick to insert under the bottom edge to lift and evenly shape the dress with inner and outer folds all the way around it.

9. Turn the doll cake base around until you decide which side you want to be the front of the doll cake.

10. Insert your doll pick down into the top of the dress to meet the fondant or buttercream. If the doll pick wobbles, remove it and add a small piece of fondant or cut marshmallow to the hole. Re-insert your doll into the center of that fondant or marshmallow and press down until her bodice reaches the top of the doll cake.

11. Finish decorating your doll cake as instructed in the doll picture.

WHITE BRIDAL DOLL DRESS

You Will Need:

Doll cake baked in Wilton Wonder Mold cake pan
1/2 recipe buttercream frosting
2 lbs white fondant
Wilton Doll Pick
Icing Tip 3
Tweezers
Super Pearl Luster Dust
Lemon Extract
Shimmering Petals Ivory Flower Pick (Amscan)
Fashion Accessories 6122504 4-piece connector
One small rhinestone
(3) 10" cake board each turned with the lines in opposite directions and
     covered in Fanci Foil wrap or a beautiful cake plate

INSTRUCTIONS:

1. Follow basic doll cake instructions 1-11.

2. Cut a 2" x 5-1/2" strip of white fondant and fit around bodice. Use tip 3 to lightly move the center of the bodice down as shown in the picture.

3. Paint entire bodice and dress with a mixture of Super Pearl Luster dust mixed with lemon extract to form liquid paint. Let dry.

4. Cut the endings off two of the jewels with snippers. Add 3 jewels to the bottom of the bodice with a dab of buttercream on the bottom of each. The center piece still has the circle opening on the end. Add rhinestone to the center.

5. Wrap flower pick around doll hair.

4

BLACK DOLL DRESS

You Will Need:

Doll cake baked in Wilton Wonder Mold cake pan
(3) 10" cake board each turned with the lines in opposite directions and
    covered in Fanci Foil wrap or a beautiful cake plate
1 recipe black buttercream frosting
    (Note: I used chocolate frosting and black gel)
Tip 21
Small daisy cutter
2 oz. black fondant
Pearls on a string
Wilton Doll Pick
Black edible glitter

INSTRUCTIONS:

1. Follow doll cake instructions 1-11.

2. Using tip 21, make black buttercream swirls all around the doll cake. I start from the bottom and fill in the entire cake.

3. Insert doll pick. Roll out black fondant. Use daisy cutter to cut out flowers to cover the bodice as shown in the picture. (Note: When attaching flowers to bodice, slightly press the soft fondant flowers into the bodice. If you have problems getting them to stick, apply a dab of water on the back of the flower.)

4. Sprinkle black edible glitter over the doll cake.

5. Wrap pearls around doll hair. Take end of pearls and tuck underneath another section of pearls to secure them.

GRAY DOLL DRESS

You Will Need:

Doll cake baked in Wilton Wonder Mold cake pan
(3) 10" cake board each turned with the lines in opposite directions and
    covered in Fanci Foil wrap or a beautiful cake plate
1 recipe gray buttercream frosting
Tips 352, 366
Gray colored sprinkles
Wilton Doll Pick
Small white roses bouquet

INSTRUCTIONS:

1. Follow doll cake instructions 1-4.

2. Using tip 366, make 9 rows of zig zag ruffles starting from the bottom of the doll cake.

3. Holding the doll pick upside down, make 5 rows of zig zag ruffles over the bodice using tip 352.

4. Insert doll pick into the top of the cake.

5. Sprinkle gray colored sugar over the doll cake.

6. Wrap flower pick around doll hair.

WEDGEWOOD BLUE DOLL DRESS

You Will Need:

Doll cake baked in Wilton Wonder Mold cake pan
1 recipe white buttercream frosting
Tip 21
Large Petal Tip 127D
(3) 10" cake board each turned with the lines in opposite directions and
  covered in Fanci Foil wrap or a beautiful cake plate
Wedgewood Blue paste color
Wilton Doll Pick

INSTRUCTIONS:

1. Follow basic doll cake instructions 1-4.

2. Use tip 127D to pipe a strip of frosting on the right side (start from the left if you're right handed) of the skirt making a swirl in the frosting at the bottom of the dress. This will mark your beginning and end point. Continue to make large swirls with tip 127D from left to right (or right to left if you're right handed) around the doll skirt. Practice on a plate before beginning so that you get the deep swirls.

3. Use tip 21 to make bodice design lines in the front.

GOLD DOLL DRESS

You Will Need:

Doll cake baked in Wilton Wonder Mold cake pan
(3) 10" cake board each turned with the lines in opposite directions and
     covered in Fanci Foil wrap or a beautiful cake plate
1/2 recipe buttercream frosting
Wilton Doll Pick
Gold Gel Paste Color
Large Rose Petal cutter
Tip 3

INSTRUCTIONS:

1. Follow basic doll cake instructions 1-11.

2. Use bodice template to cut bodice pattern out of fondant. Fold fondant into pleats in the upper right corner and apply to fondant covered cake. Use tip 3 to imprint 3 circles as shown in the picture.

3. For the side of the dress and the flower, use the large rose petal cutter to cut out petals and pinch the edges together. Attach them with piping gel and overlap and turn as shown in the picture.

4. Add the 5 petal flower to the other side of the dress. Take a small piece of fondant and make centers for both flowers.

MINI DOLL CAKES

These miniature doll cakes are perfect one serving desserts. I have given these to women on birthdays and other special occasions. These cakes would make perfect gifts for maid of honor and bridesmaids. I would suggest you practice making the mini doll cakes before making a regular doll cake if you have never made the large doll cake.

MINI DOLL CAKE INSTRUCTIONS

You Will Need:

Miniature doll cake baked in Wilton Mini Wonder Mold cake pan
1/4 - 1/2 cups buttercream frosting
5 oz. fondant
Mini Doll Pick
Waxed Paper Square or 3" cake circle

INSTRUCTIONS:

1. Bake your cake recipe in the Mini Wonder Mold cake pan using a large cookie scoop to put the batter in each cavity. This is the easiest way to fill these pans. Once the cakes have been baked, turn them out to release them, and move to a cooling rack.

2. Set miniature doll cake on a wax paper square. Cut the cake so that it has two layers.

3. Put frosting between the layers. If you choose to add a filling, place a dam of frosting around the edge of the cake to hold the filling inside the cake.

4. Apply a layer of frosting to the entire cake and place in the refrigerator so that the frosting can set.

5. When you remove the chilled cake from the refrigerator, smooth the frosting with a paper towel.

6. Roll out the fondant into a circle. If you want to use the impression mat, do it now. Use even pressure all across the mat so your design will be even with no gaps. Use a 6" cake board and a pizza cutter to cut out the fondant and then smooth the cut edge with your finger.

7. Lift the fondant onto your cold doll cake base making sure that you center it evenly over the doll. I usually eye ball it.

8. Gently smooth the fondant to make sure that the fondant has good contact with the buttercream frosting. As you smooth the fondant dress, the bottom of the skirt will go into gentle curves. Use your fingers under the bottom edge to shape the dress to add even inner and outer folds.

9. Turn the doll cake base around until you decide which side you want to be the front of the doll cake.

10. Press your doll pick into the top part of the dress and follow instructions to make your favorite mini doll cake.

YELLOW MINI DOLL DRESS

You Will Need:

Doll cake baked in Wilton Mini Wonder Mold cake pan
1/4 cup buttercream frosting
6 oz. yellow fondant
Mini Doll Pick
Rubber Stampede's Geometric Swirl Background (3314R)

INSTRUCTIONS:

1. Follow Mini Doll instructions 1-6, using the Geometric stamp to emboss the fondant and then continue following instructions 7-10.

2. Cut a plain piece of yellow fondant 1-1/2" x 3", fold down the top part slightly and wrap around doll bodice. Trim excess off the back. Press seam together.

P U R P L E M I N I D O L L D R E S S

You Will Need:

Doll cake baked in Wilton Mini Wonder Mold cake pan
1/4 cup buttercream frosting
Tip 3
Stampalicious Cube
Wilton Crinkle Heart Cutter
6 oz. purple fondant
Mini Doll Pick
Piping gel

INSTRUCTIONS:

1. Follow Mini Doll instructions 1-10. Before applying fondant skirt to doll cake, imprint it with Stampalicious cube lace as shown in the picture.

2. Cut 4 crinkle hearts out of purple fondant. Center one over the bust area and then add two to either side of the center wrapping the hearts around to the back. Attach the final heart on the back of the bodice. Imprint with tip 3 circles as shown in the picture.

GREEN MINI DOLL DRESS

You Will Need:

Doll cake baked in Wilton Mini Wonder Mold cake pan
1/4 cup buttercream frosting
6 oz. green fondant
Mini Doll Pick
Floral Impression Mat (CK)
Wilton Large Leaf Petal Cutter
Tip 3
Piping gel

INSTRUCTIONS:

1. Follow Mini Doll instructions 1-10 above, embossing the fondant with the floral impression mat before cutting the circle and applying it to the mini doll cake.

2. Cut out 2 large petal leaves. Paint the back of each leaf with piping gel, and then wrap around the bodice as shown in the picture. The large part of the leaf goes over the bodice first and then wrapped around the back. The large part of the second leaf gets wrapped from the back with the tail end being wrapped around the front.

BROWN MINI DOLL DRESS

You Will Need:

Doll cake baked in Wilton Mini Wonder Mold cake pan
1/4 cup buttercream frosting
6 oz. chocolate fondant
Wilton Square Crinkle Cutter
Small Tear drop Crinkle Cutter
Mini Doll Pick
Piping gel

INSTRUCTIONS:

1. Follow Mini Doll instructions 1-10.

2. Cut out square using crinkle cutter. Turn the square so that it looks like a diamond and, using the same cutter, take a piece out of the top and sides to make room for the neckline and the arms. Wrap it around the doll bodice shaping the top to make it a v-neck.

3. Roll out fondant. Cut a teardrop shape using the small crinkle cutter. Wrap it around the doll as shown in the picture.

RED MINI DOLL DRESS

You Will Need:

Doll cake baked in Wilton Mini Wonder Mold cake pan
1/4 cup buttercream frosting
6 oz. red fondant
Mini Doll Pick
Small Rose Petal cutter
Super Pearl Luster Dust
Lemon Extract
Paint Brush

INSTRUCTIONS:

1. Follow Mini Doll instructions 1-10.

2. Cut out 11 petals using cutter and apply to bodice as shown in the picture. The petals wrap around the back of the bodice as well and the last one is placed under the petals in the front.

3. Paint entire dress with a mixture of Super Pearl Luster dust and lemon extract.

Dress Cookie Hearts

These dress cookie hearts can be made in many sizes to suit your event. I've used various colors that could also be customized for your party or recipient's favorite color.

Purple Heart Shaped Dress Cookie

You will need:

1 heart sugar cookie
Piping gel
5 oz. purple fondant
Heart cookie cutter
PME Open Vee Crimper
Paint brush

Instructions:

1. Cut out fondant with heart cookie cutter.

2. Paint cookie with piping gel. Roll out fondant to 1/4 inch and set on cookie. Gently smooth top.

3. Starting with right side of heart, start crimping fondant to make 3 diagonal rows from right to left. Finish crimping left side of heart as shown in the picture.

CHAMPAGNE HEART SHAPED
DRESS COOKIE

You will need:

1 heart sugar cookie
Piping gel
4 oz. pink fondant
Heart cookie cutter
Champagne Luster Dust
Lemon extract
Paint brush
Wilton Designer Pattern Press Set
 - Corner Flourish press

INSTRUCTIONS:

1. Cut out fondant with heart cookie cutter.

2. Paint cookie with piping gel. Roll out fondant and set on cookie. Gently smooth top.

3. Starting from the bottom of the heart, press the corner flourish pattern into the fondant 3 times, overlapping each one as shown in picture.

4. Using a dry paint brush, mix together a little lemon extract with the Champagne luster dust.

5. Paint the entire bodice.

6. Let dry.

WHITE HEART SHAPED DRESS COOKIE

You will need:

1 heart sugar cookie
Piping gel
Paint Brush
4 oz. white fondant
Super Pearl Luster Dust
White sugar crystals
Heart cookie cutter
Large Daisy flower cutter
Tip 1E

INSTRUCTIONS:

1. Cut out fondant with heart cookie cutter.

2. Paint cookie with piping gel. Roll out fondant and set on cookie. Gently smooth top.

3. Move down slightly and lightly imprint the top part of the heart to create the bodice separation.

4. Using a dry paint brush, dust the top part of the bodice with Super Pearl luster dust.

5. Paint the bottom part of the bodice with piping gel and then fill area with white sugar crystals.

6. Add large daisy flower to the cookie. Imprint with tip 1E. Let dry.

Dress Cookies

These dress cookies have been shipped all over the United States this year to be part of birthday celebrations, bridal showers and a host of other parties for women. The sky is really the limit when designing these cookies.

Dress Cookie Instructions:

You will need:

1 batch sugar cookie recipe
Dress cookie cutter
Piping gel
Paint brush
2 oz. fondant in your favorite color
Tools specific to the design (see below)

Instructions:

1. Use your favorite sugar cookie recipe and the dress cookie cutter to cut out the cookies.

2. Place about 2" apart on the parchment lined cookie sheet. Bake at 350 degrees until golden brown. Cool.

3. Follow instructions below for your favorite design.

Orange – Roll out orange fondant. Cut out the dress and apply it to the cookie with piping gel. Cut 4 small blossoms and attach to bodice as shown in the picture.

Baby Blue – Roll out baby blue fondant. Cut out the dress and apply it to the cookie with piping gel. Use the Symmetrical Swirl press from Wilton's Designer Pattern Press Set to emboss the dress 3 times as shown in the picture.

Green – Roll out green fondant. Cut out the dress and apply it to the cookie with piping gel. Use the Corner Flourish press from Wilton's Designer Pattern Press Set to emboss the dress bodice twice as shown in the picture. Use small leave cutter to make 30 leaves and attach each to dress with piping gel overlapping each row as shown in the picture. Dust entire dress with Holly Green luster dust.

Yellow – Roll out yellow fondant. Cut out the dress and apply it to the cookie with piping gel. Use a 5-star flower cutter to lightly press 3 flowers in the fondant as shown in the picture. Use the stitching tool to make the pattern shown in the picture.

Pink – Roll out pink fondant. Cut out the dress and apply it to the cookie with piping gel. Use the Flower press from Wilton's Designer Pattern Press Set to emboss the dress as shown in the picture. Use the end of your gum paste star pointed tip tool, turn the dots in the center to stars. Follow picture design to add stars to the inside of the end pattern.

Aqua – Roll out aqua fondant. Cut out the dress and apply it to the cookie with piping gel. Use the Vine press from Wilton's Designer Pattern Press Set to emboss the dress as shown in the picture. Cut out 5 small fondant daisy flowers and attach to the cookie as shown with piping gel. Use tip 2C to emboss the center of each flower.

Light Turquoise – Roll out light turquoise fondant. Cut out the dress and apply it to the cookie with piping gel. Use tip 81 to lightly press design into bodice and dress bottom as shown in the picture.

Dark Purple – Roll out dark purple fondant. Cut out the dress and apply it to the cookie with piping gel. Use the Corner Flourish press from Wilton's Designer Pattern Press Set to emboss the dress as shown in the picture. Add 6 medium sized blossoms to the dress.

Red – Roll out red fondant. Use Stampalicious cube lace side to imprint lace all over fondant. Cut out the dress and apply it to the cookie with piping gel. Dust with Super Pearl luster dust.

Burgundy – Roll out burgundy fondant. Use CK's Flower Fun texture sheet to emboss dress. Cut out the dress and apply it to the cookie with piping gel.

Blue – Roll out blue fondant. Cut out the dress and apply to the cookie with piping gel. Use the Flower press from Wilton's Designer Pattern Press Set to emboss the dress as shown in the picture. Dust with Super Pearl luster dust.

Ivory – Roll out ivory fondant. Cut out the dress and apply it to the cookie with piping gel. Use stitching tool to make stitching lines in fondant. Attach small blossoms in sets of two as shown in the picture.

Brown – Roll out chocolate fondant. Cut out the dress and apply it to the cookie with piping gel. Use the Curlicues press from Wilton's Designer Pattern Press Set to emboss the dress. Dust with Super Pearl luster dust.

Purple – Roll out purple fondant. Cut out the dress and apply it to the cookie with piping gel. Use the Quilting Patchwork cutter to diagonally emboss the dress as shown in the picture. Fill in the bottom part of the dress with small blossoms as shown in the picture.

White – Roll out white fondant. Cut out the dress and attach to your cookie with piping gel. Use a small piece of chocolate fondant to make ribbon band and a bow using the template in Chapter 13. Attach with piping gel. Dust with Super Pearl luster dust.

Chapter 2
SHOES & BOOTS

CHOCOLATE SHOES

Want to make a shoe lover's day? Make them a chocolate shoe in their favorite color. The molds for these shoes are in two parts. You can make them as shown or for the more advanced artists, please check out Jennifer Dontz's website – www.jenniferdontz.com – for instructions on how to make a stand up shoe.

GREEN CHOCOLATE SHOE

You will need:

1 – 14 oz. bag of Green Candy Melts
4" Shoe Mold (see Suppliers/Favorite Websites)
Sharp Knife
Clear Piping gel
White cotton gloves
4 oz. green fondant or candy clay
Large Daisy cutter
Wax Paper

INSTRUCTIONS:

1. Melt 14 oz. bag of Green Candy Melts using a double boiler or in the microwave following instructions on the bag. Stir until completely smooth.

2. Make sure that your mold is completely dry and free of any grease. Fill cavity of 4" mold with melted chocolate. Gently tap the bottom of the mold to remove all air bubbles. Lift mold up to see if there are any remaining bubbles.

3. Take a bench scraper or spatula to completely smooth the top.

4. Set the mold into a rectangular container so that it stays level. Place in the refrigerator to set. I normally let it stay in there for 4 or more hours.

5. After removing the mold from the refrigerator, use a piece of wax paper to unmold the shoe onto. Use your white cotton gloves to handle the shoe so you won't leave any marks on it.

6. Use a sharp knife to trim excess chocolate from the edges.

7. Using piping gel, paint small sections of the shoe, cut out green fondant (or candy clay) daisies, and attach to the shoe. Continue until shoe is completely covered.

8. Let set until dry.

WHITE CHOCOLATE SHOE

You will need:

1 – 14 oz. bag of White Candy Melts
4" Shoe Mold (see Suppliers/Favorite Websites)
Sharp Knife
Clear Piping gel

White cotton gloves
White Edible Glitter
Wax Paper

INSTRUCTIONS:

1. Melt 14 oz. bag of White Candy Melts using a double boiler or in the microwave following instructions on the bag. Stir until completely smooth.

2. Make sure that your mold is completely dry and free of any grease. Fill cavity of 4" mold with melted chocolate. Gently tap the bottom of the mold to remove all air bubbles. Lift mold up to see if there are any remaining bubbles.

3. Take a bench scraper or spatula to completely smooth the top.

4. Set the mold into a rectangular container so that it stays level. Place in the refrigerator to set. I normally let it stay in there for 4 or more hours.

5. After removing the mold from the refrigerator, use a piece of wax paper to unmold the shoe onto. Use your white cotton gloves to handle the shoe so you won't leave any marks on it.

6. Use a sharp knife to trim excess chocolate from the edges.

7. Using a large paint brush and long strokes, paint shoe section with clear piping gel.

8. Sprinkle white edible glitter all over shoe. Gently press in to make sure it makes contact all over the shoe.

9. Let set until dry.

PINK CHOCOLATE SHOE

You will need:

1 – 14 oz. bag of Pink Candy Melts
4" Shoe Mold (see Suppliers/Favorite Websites)
Sharp Knife

White cotton gloves
White Stokes Clear Glitter Piping gel
Wax Paper

INSTRUCTIONS:

1. Melt 14 oz. bag of Pink Candy Melts using a double boiler or in the microwave following instructions on the bag. Stir until completely smooth.

2. Make sure that your mold is completely dry and free of any grease. Fill cavity of 4" mold with melted chocolate. Gently tap the bottom of the mold to remove all air bubbles. Lift mold up to see if there are any remaining bubbles.

3. Take a bench scraper or spatula to completely smooth the top.

4. Set the mold into a rectangular container so that it stays level. Place in the refrigerator to set. I normally let it stay in there for 4 or more hours.

5. After removing the mold from the refrigerator, use a piece of wax paper to unmold the shoe onto. Use your white cotton gloves to handle the shoe so you won't leave any marks on it.

6. Use a sharp knife to trim excess chocolate from the edges.

7. Using a large paint brush and long strokes, paint shoe section with white glitter piping gel.

8. Let set until dry.

RED CHOCOLATE SHOE

You will need:

1 – 14 oz. bag of Red Candy Melts
4" Shoe Mold (see Suppliers/Favorite Websites)
Sharp Knife
White cotton gloves
Clear Piping gel
Gold Pearlized Sugar Sprinkles
Wax Paper

INSTRUCTIONS:

1. Melt 14 oz. bag of Red Candy Melts using a double boiler or in the microwave following instructions on the bag. Stir until completely smooth.

2. Make sure that your mold is completely dry and free of any grease. Fill cavity of 4" mold with melted chocolate. Gently tap the bottom of the mold to remove all air bubbles. Lift mold up to see if there are any remaining bubbles.

3. Take a bench scraper or spatula to completely smooth the top.

4. Set the mold into a rectangular container so that it stays level. Place in the refrigerator to set. I normally let it stay in there for 4 or more hours.

5. After removing the mold from the refrigerator, use a piece of wax paper to unmold the shoe onto. Use your white cotton gloves to handle the shoe so you won't leave any marks on it.

6. Use a sharp knife to trim excess chocolate from the edges.

7. Using a large paint brush and long strokes, paint shoe section with clear piping gel.

8. Sprinkle gold pearlized sugar sprinkles all over shoe. Gently press in to make sure it makes contact all over the shoe.

9. Let set until dry.

SHOE COOKIES

Surprisingly, shoe cookies are my second most requested cookie. For Marcella Stafford and all of my other shoe lovers, these are for you.

You will need:

1 batch sugar cookie recipe
Shoe cookie cutter
Piping gel
3 oz. Fondant or candy clay in your favorite color
Tools specific to the design (see below)

INSTRUCTIONS:

1. Bake sugar cookies using the shoe cookie cutter. Let completely cool.

2. Paint sugar cookie with a thin layer of piping gel.

3. Follow instructions below for your favorite shoe.

Fuchsia – Roll out fuchsia fondant. Use shoe cutter to cut out fondant shoe. Attach to cookie with piping gel. Use Wilton Decorating Comb to press into fondant at a 45 degree angle spaced apart as shown in the picture. Use tip 2 to make indentations on top of shoe.

Black – Roll out black fondant. Use shoe cutter to cut out fondant shoe. Attach to cookie with piping gel. Lay Designer Stencils C149-Rosette on top of fondant. Lightly roll over stencil with rolling pin to secure it to the top. Dust with Nu Silver luster dust. Remove stencil.

White Pearl – Roll out white fondant. Use shoe cutter to cut out fondant shoe. Attach to cookie with piping gel. Use pizza cutter to gently mark a line in the fondant to separate top section of the shoe from the bottom section. Paint the bottom section with piping gel. Sprinkle white sugar glitter over shoe. Paint top part of shoe with piping gel and cover with ivory sugar pearls. Use a knife to line pearls up together.

Gold – Roll out gold fondant. Use shoe cutter to cut out fondant shoe. Attach to cookie with piping gel. Use Symmetrical Swirl press from Wilton's Designer Pattern Press Set to emboss design 4 times on shoe as shown in the picture.

Mint Green – Roll out mint green fondant. Use shoe cutter to cut out fondant shoe. Attach to cookie with piping gel. Cut out mint green blossoms and attach to the shoe overlapping as shown in the picture.

White Bridal – Roll out white fondant. Use shoe cutter to cut out fondant shoe. Attach to cookie with piping gel. Use Stampalicious cube to lightly imprint design twice like shown in the picture. Dust with Super Pearl luster dust.

Purple – Roll out purple fondant. Emboss with paisley impression sheet. Use shoe cutter to cut out fondant shoe. Attach to cookie with piping gel. Paint with Super Pearl luster dust.

Blue – Roll out blue fondant. Use shoe cutter to cut out fondant shoe. Attach to cookie with piping gel. Use the Flower press from Wilton's Designer Pattern Press Set to emboss the shoe twice as shown in the picture.

Brown – Roll out chocolate fondant. Emboss with animal print. Use shoe cutter to cut out fondant shoe. Attach to cookie with piping gel. Paint with Super Pearl luster dust.

Aqua – Roll out aqua fondant. Use shoe cutter to cut out fondant shoe. Attach to cookie with piping gel. Use Stitching tool to make lines in fondant. Cut a triangle piece of fondant and attach to shoe as shown. Make indentations on shoe with a toothpick.

Pink – Roll out pink fondant. Use shoe cutter to cut out fondant shoe. Attach to cookie with piping gel. Press large daisies all over fondant. Use tip 1E to imprint center of flowers.

Golden Yellow – Roll out golden yellow fondant. Emboss with large animal print. Use shoe cutter to cut out fondant shoe. Attach to cookie with piping gel.

SNOW BOOT CAKE

I love this cake because it is easy to make. Your kids can help you press the coconut into the frosting and add the chocolate jewels.

You will need:

1 – 13x9x2 Cake
6 cups white buttercream
5 oz. white fondant or candy clay
1– 14oz. bag coconut
Tip 21
Large Petal Tip 127D

Jewel Candy Mold (CK 90-5124)
White Candy Melt disks
White Edible Glitter
Paint Brush
Super Pearl Luster dust
Boot template

INSTRUCTIONS:

1. Make 3 white diamonds using the jewel candy mold. Dust with Super Pearl luster dust. Set aside.

2. Enlarge the boot template 225%, cut it out and turn over to use as a template it to cut your cake.

3. Completely frost the top of your cake with buttercream frosting. Add tip 21 swirls to the sole of your boot, the top, right side and heel of your boot.

4. Apply coconut to the top and left border of the boot. Press the coconut into the cake to make sure it adhers to the buttercream frosting.

5. Add three layers of tip 127D fans to right side of boot starting from the bottom up as shown in the picture.

6. Press white diamonds into buttercream as shown.

7. Sprinkle top of boot with white edible glitter.

LEATHER BOOT CAKE

You will need:

1 – 13x9x2 Sheet Cake
2 cups chocolate buttercream
3-1/2 - 4 lbs chocolate fondant or candy clay
6 oz. tan fondant or candy clay
Large animal print press
Pointed end tool
Brown gel color

Pizza cutter
Wilton Large Leaf cutter
Vodka
Paint brush
Piping gel
Leather Boot template

INSTRUCTIONS:

1. Cut the dome off your sheet cake. Put it cut side down onto your cake board or serving platter.

2. Enlarge leather boot template to 225% and use it to cut your cake.

3. Use buttercream frosting to cover the cake completely. Refrigerate until frosting is set.

4. Roll chocolate fondant out 1/4" thick. Use the animal print embosser, press into fondant in sections making sure you don't overlap the previous section.

5. Lift and gently apply to boot smoothing it over the edges to make sure it has complete contact with the buttercream underneath.

6. Trim excess fondant at an angle so the edges are smooth.

7. Use tan fondant and cut a strip of fondant 2" x 9". Paint the back of the fondant with piping gel. Apply to top of boot as shown in picture.

8. Cut out 3 large leaves, add piping gel to the backs and attach to the boot as shown in the picture.

9. Use a pointed tool to emboss the band and the leaves as shown in the picture.

10. Use a little brown gel and vodka to make a paint and use paint brush to paint over entire boot.

BOOT COOKIES

I couldn't resist adding these cut little boot cookies to the book. Let your imagination run wild coming up with even more designs.

You will need:

1 batch sugar cookie recipe
Boot cookie template
Piping gel
4 oz. Fondant or candy clay in your favorite color
Tools specific to the design (see below)

INSTRUCTIONS:

1. Bake sugar cookies using the boot cookie template. Let completely cool.

2. Paint sugar cookie with a thin layer of piping gel.

3. Follow instructions below for your favorite boot.

Brown – Roll out chocolate fondant. Use boot cookie template to cut out fondant and attach to piping gel covered cookie. Use Wilton's Designer Pattern Press Set, Curlicues press to imprint design on boot as shown in picture. Use paring knife to create lines for sole and heel.

Red – Roll out red fondant. Use boot cookie template to cut out fondant and attach to piping gel covered cookie. Use stitching tool to make design on boot. Cut out 6 small blossom flowers and attach to cookie as shown in the picture. Use paring knife to create lines for heel.

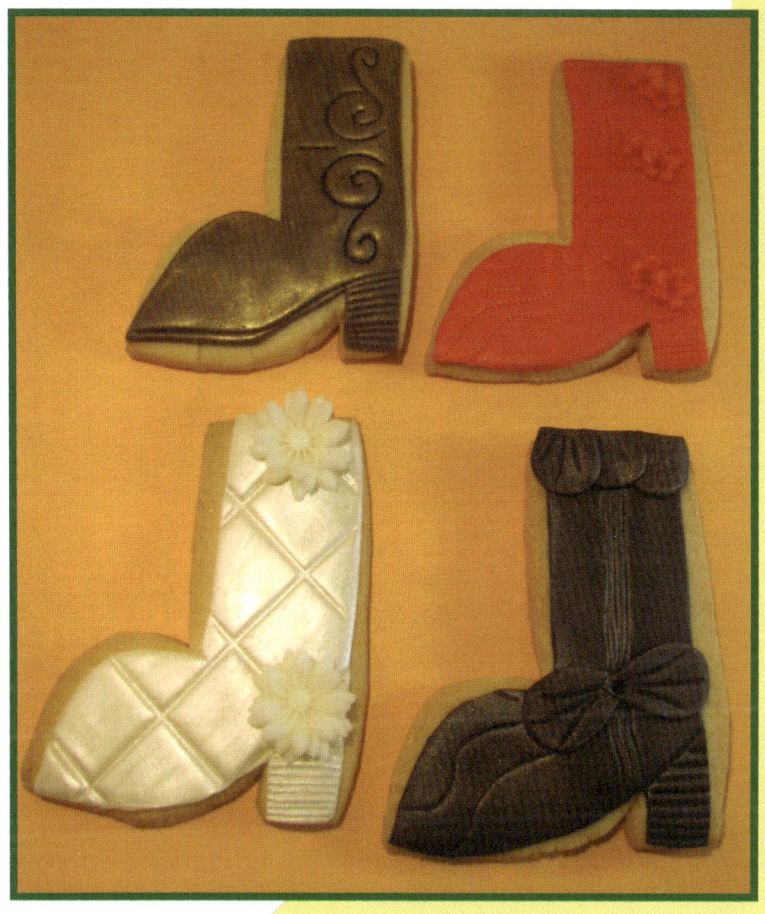

White – Roll out white fondant. Use Earlene Moore's 1" diamond impression mat to emboss fondant as shown in the picture. Use boot cookie template to cut out fondant and attach to piping gel covered cookie. Dust with Super Pearl Luster dust mixed with lemon extract. Attach two small daisy cutter flowers to top and bottom of boot and emboss center with tip 2C. Use paring knife to create lines for heel.

Black – Roll out black fondant. Use boot cookie template to cut out fondant and attach to piping gel covered cookie. Use rose petal cutter to cut out 5 petals. Attach to cookie as shown in the picture. Emboss with small roller. Use paring knife to create lines for heel.

29

Chapter 3
HATS

These hats are dedicated to my wonderful mother, Jannie Mosely, my aunts – Annice Jones, Clarice Birney, Estella Robinson, Susie Robinson, Rosie Abram, Gayzell Mosely, and my dear friends Carolyn Fleming-Williams and Margaret Davis because they all look incredible in hats. Make these hat cookies for church socials and meetings, for special bridal showers, for birthdays or any other time you want to make someone smile.

MINI HAT CUPCAKES

You will need:

Ice Cream cupcake pan
1/4 cups buttercream frosting
6 oz. fondant
Piping gel
Paint brush
Wax paper square or 3" cake board

INSTRUCTIONS:

1. Use Crisco and flour to grease and flour your ice cream cupcake pan. Bake your favorite pound cake recipe in the pans, filling no more than 2/3 full. I find it easy to fill these pans with a large cookie scoop.

2. Let cool completely and trim excess crown off top. Invert onto wax paper square or 3" cake board with a dab of frosting.

3. Lightly frost the ice cream cupcake. Refrigerate until frosting has set.

4. If you want to have an extra treat, dip the bottoms of your ice cream cupcakes into melted chocolate and set on waxed paper until set. Trim excess chocolate.

5. Follow instructions below for your favorite design.

Green – Roll out green fondant. Cover cold ice cream cupcake. Trim excess fondant from base at a 45 degree angle so that the fondant goes under the hat. Cut 3 large leaves and imprint center with the Flower press from Wilton's Designer Pattern Press Set. Attach to the hat as shown in the picture. Add a fondant center.

Orange – Roll out orange fondant. Cover cold ice cream cupcake. Trim excess fondant from base at a 45 degree angle so that the fondant goes under the hat.

Purple – Roll out purple fondant. Cover cold ice cream cupcake. Trim excess fondant from base at a 45 degree angle so that the fondant goes under the hat. Cut two triangles from Wilton's Crinkle Cutter set. Attach to hat. Cut out a flower and attach to the center of the triangles. Imprint center with tip 1C.

White – Use white buttercream frosting and tip 86 to create a ruffle on a plain ice cream cupcake. Fill in the rest of the cupcake with tip 21 stars. Use tip 352 to create 3 leaves as shown in the picture. Attach 7 ivory sugar pearls to center of leaves.

Aqua – Roll out aqua fondant. Cover cold ice cream cupcake. Trim excess fondant from base at a 45 degree angle so that the fondant goes under the hat. Cut 8 leaves and fan around the front of the hat leaving space in the middle. Cut 2 flowers using the large blossom cutter. Attach each to the hat alternating the petals. Imprint center of flower with star tool.

MINI HAT COOKIES

You will need:

1 Hat Sugar Cookie
Piping gel
5 oz. fondant
Hat template
Specific tools listed below

INSTRUCTIONS:

1. Use your favorite sugar cookie recipe and the hat template to cut out the cookies.

2. Bake on parchment lined cookie pans at 350 degrees until golden brown. Cool. Paint with piping gel.

3. Follow design instructions below.

Baby Blue – Roll out baby blue fondant. Use Earlene Moore's diamond impression mat to imprint part of the fondant. Use the template to cut out the hat with the top part showing the diamond imprint and the hat band fondant smooth. Attach to piping gel covered cookie. Cut a 1/2" x 3.5" and 1/2" x 2" band for the brim overlapping on left side of hat. Add 5 fondant petals to hat with piping gel and make a fondant center.

Brown – Roll out chocolate fondant. Use template to cut out hat. Attach to piping gel covered cookie. Roll out chocolate fondant and emboss with animal print. Cut 4" x 2-1/2" strip of fondant at an angle making the end piece 2" wide as shown in picture. Attach to cookie with piping gel.

Peach – Roll out peach fondant. Use template to cut out hat. Attach to piping gel covered cookie. Lay Designer Stencils C005 Victorian Scroll stencil over fondant as shown in picture. Press rolling pin over stencil to make sure it adheres to the fondant. Use Sunlit Cactus Luster Dust and a paint brush or sponge to apply color over the stencil design. Gently remove stencil.

Black/White – Cut out 10 (1-1/2" x 1-1/2") squares in both white and black fondant. Lay on piping gel covered cookie in a checkerboard fashion. Gently roll over design to blend the squares together. Set hat template over fondant design and cut away excess fondant. Cut out 8 small white fondant hearts and attach to inner seams as shown in picture.

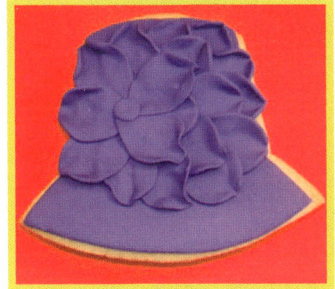

Purple – Roll out purple fondant. Use hat template to cut out the fondant. Lay on piping gel covered cookie. Cover top part of hat with rose petals with the tips folded over partially. Start putting the petals on the hat from the right top part of the hat to the left. Use picture to follow design pattern. Make a small fondant circle to cover petal edge. Pat down to smooth.

Fuchsia – Roll out fuchsia fondant. Cut out hat template. Lay on piping gel covered cookie. Use the Corner Flourish press from Wilton's Designer Pattern Press Set to emboss the fondant three times starting from right to left, slightly overlapping the previous design. Take the press off the right side of the hat to make the half imprint as shown in picture. Add 3 fondant daisies with a dab of piping gel. Press tip 1E into the centers.

Aqua – Roll out aqua fondant. Cut out hat template. Lay on piping gel covered cookie. Use Wilton swirl press roller to emboss top part of hat leaving the brim smooth. Use Wilton's Designer Press Set, Symmetrical Swirl to emboss the hat band. Cut out 3 small crinkle cutter teardrops and attach as shown in the picture with piping gel. Use tip 1E to emboss the centers of the swirls and the top of the teardrop.

Mint Green – Roll out mint green fondant. Apply a thin layer of piping gel to cookie. Use template to cut out hat and then emboss the top section of the hat with the Quilting Patchwork cutter. Gently apply fondant over cookie. Cut out a 1/2" x 4" band of mint green fondant. Apply a thin stripe of piping gel around the bottom of the quilted design and apply the band. Trim excess fondant from cookie. Cut 1-inch strips of fondant in 3 various lengths. Fold in half and apply to cookie as shown in the picture. The last strip should come off the cookie slightly. With your scissors, make a point on the longer tail.

Gold – Roll out gold fondant. Use hat template to cut out the fondant. Paint piping gel on cookie and attach the fondant. Lightly mark off 1/2" sections of the hat as shown in picture using your pizza cutter. Paint those sections with piping gel and then add sugar crystals. Let set until dry. Remove excess crystals. Use the large leaf petal template to cut out 3 gold leaves. Fold over the edge and attach to the cookie with piping gel as shown in the picture.

White – Roll out white fondant. Use Rubber Stampede's Geometric Swirl Background (3314R) to make the impression on the top part of the hat. Cut out hat template. Apply piping gel to cookie and attach fondant. Cut out 9 fondant leaves and add to brim as shown in the picture. Dust with Super Pearl Luster Dust.

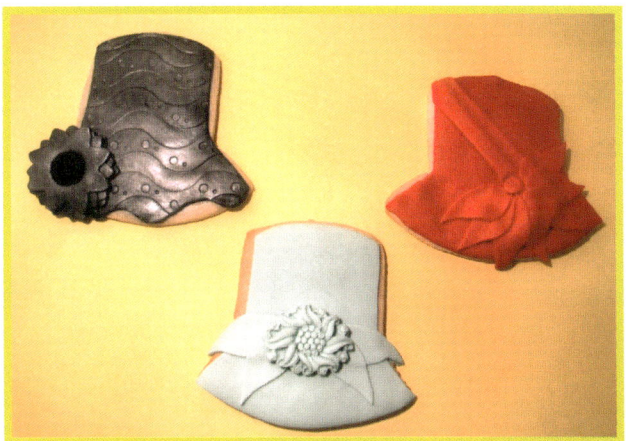

Black Flower – Roll out black fondant. Use CK's Wavy Dots texture sheet to emboss the fondant. Apply a thin layer of piping gel to the cookie. Cut out hat template top and sides. For the bottom, use your knife or fondant tool to make a wavy brim. Gently apply fondant cut out to cookie. Paint cookie with Nu Silver Luster Dust. Cut out 4 large fondant flowers, paint each with Nu Silver Luster Dust and attach them with piping gel to cookie alternating each flower as shown in picture. Press down the center of the top flower and attach a marble sized piece of black fondant to the center. Paint center piece with piping gel and apply black non-pareils. Let dry. Remove excess.

Red – Roll out red fondant. Apply a thin layer of piping gel to cookie. Use template to cut out hat. Gently apply fondant over cookie. Paint a thin diagonal stripe of piping gel on the fondant. Cut a 3/4" x 6" strip of red fondant and apply it to the cookie like shown in the picture. Using Wilton's Leaf Cutter set to cut out 7 medium sized fondant leaves and apply each leaf with piping gel as shown in the picture. Use tip 1E to imprint the center of the half flower. Roll a pea sized amount of red fondant and press over the impression.

Light Turquoise – Use an ounce of light turquoise fondant to fill a silicone broach mold. Remove and trim excess fondant. Set aside. Roll out light turquoise fondant. Use hat template to cut out the fondant. Paint piping gel on cookie and gently attach the fondant. Cut out 4 large leaves (2 one way and 2 in the opposite direction). Attach with piping gel as shown in the picture. Paint the back of the broach with piping gel and apply it to the center of the hat. Let dry.

Chapter 4
PANTS

Pants cakes and cookies make great desserts for teens or slumber parties. Want individual desserts? Use mini loaf shape pans to make cupcakes for the pants. They can create their own designs.

GREEN PANTS CAKE

You will need:

1 – 11x7x2 Sheet Cake
1 recipe green buttercream frosting
1/4 cup white buttercream frosting
Tip 21
Super Pearl Luster Dust
Large Jewel Candy Mold (CK 90-5675)
Jewel Candy Mold (CK 90-5124)
White Candy Melt disks
Paintbrush
Pants template

INSTRUCTIONS:

1. Melt some of the white candy melts and make 8 square jewels using the small jewel candy mold. Make 1 large rectangular jewel using the large jewel candy mold. Dust with Super Pearl luster dust. Set aside.

2. Enlarge pants template 200%. Using tip 21, make green buttercream stars all over the pants section.

3. Make white buttercream stars as shown in the picture.

4. Add large and small candy jewels to the pants as shown in the picture.

BLUE & WHITE PANTS CAKE

You will need:

1 – 11x7x2 Sheet Cake
1/2 recipe white buttercream frosting
1-1/4 lb. white fondant
3/4 lb. baby blue fondant
Wilton Crinkle Cutter Set, Round crinkle cutter
Large Daisy Cutter
Piping gel
Tip 1E
Exacto Knife

INSTRUCTIONS:

1. Enlarge pants template 200%.

2. Frost cake and place in refrigerator to allow frosting to set. Remove from refrigerator and apply a thin layer of blue to the pants crotch/leg area as shown in the picture.

3. Cover entire cake with white fondant. Cover cake with template and use Exacto knife to cut away section as shown in the picture to reveal the blue fondant.

4. Use blue fondant to cut out 12 round crinkles for the top of the pants and apply with a dab of piping gel as shown in the picture. Cut out enough round crinkles to go around the edge of your cake.

5. Use white fondant to cut out 12 large daisies. Apply to center of blue crinkles and lightly press in the centers with tip 1E.

6. Use small rounds of fondant between the blue round crinkles as shown in the picture. Roll a piece of white fondant into a 4" rope. Coil the end and attach to the belt as shown.

PANTS COOKIES

You will need:

Pants shaped sugar cookies
Piping gel
3 oz. fondant in your favorite color
Specific tools listed below

INSTRUCTIONS:

1. Use your favorite sugar cookie recipe and a rectangular cookie cutter (4-1/2" x 3-1/2") to cut out the cookies.

2. Bake on parchment lined cookie pans at 350 degrees until golden brown. Cool.

3. Paint with piping gel.

4. Follow design instructions below.

Black – Roll out black fondant. Use animal print press to emboss the fondant. Use rectangular cookie cutter to cut out the fondant and attach to piping gel covered rectangle cookie. Take a piece of fondant and roll it into a strip and attach to waist as shown in the picture.

White – Roll out white fondant. Use rectangular cookie cutter to cut out the fondant and attach to piping gel covered cookie. Use Wilton's Designer Pattern Press, Vines press to emboss the pants as shown in the picture. Paint Super White Luster dust on outer legs and band. Attach 4 small white daisy flowers, 2 small pink daisy flowers, and 2 small yellow daisy flowers to the pants as shown in the picture and emboss centers of daisies with tip 2C. (Note: For this cookie, I cut the opening for the pants before the cookie was baked. It's easier to make the cookies without doing this.)

Brown – Roll out brown fondant. Emboss with Wilton's swirl pattern roller. Use rectangular cookie cutter to cut out the fondant and attach to piping gel covered rectangle cookie. Cut out two strips of fondant and attach to waistband criss-crossing in front as shown on the picture. Use a pointed tool to make 3 indentations at both ends of band.

Orange – Roll out orange fondant. Use CK's paisley pattern mat to emboss fondant. Cut out a rectangular piece of fondant to fit cookie and attach with piping gel. Use pizza cutter to separate the pants. Make a fondant waist band and fold over strap. Emboss band and strap with tip 1E.

Chapter 5
PURSES

I love making these cookies. The centers are cut out of these cookies, however, you can leave the centers in if you choose. For all of the purse lovers like me, these designs are for you.

RED PURSE CAKE

You Will Need:

6" round cake
3/4 cup red buttercream frosting
1 lb. red fondant
Large Daisy Flower Cutter
White sugar sprinkles
Piping gel
Paint brush
Wax Paper

Instructions:

1. Cut an end off the side of your cake so that it can stand up on its side. Make two wax paper templates – one for the front/back of your cake and a strip for the top part of your cake.

2. Completely frost the cake with buttercream frosting. Place onto serving plate and refrigerate until set.

3. Roll out fondant. Use your templates to cut out the top strip and apply it to your cake. Now cut out the front piece and attach it to your cake. Run your finger along the edges to smooth it out. Cut out the back piece and attach it to your cake. Smooth the edges.

4. Cut two rectangle pieces of fondant 3"x 2" and cut one end of each piece into a point as shown in the picture. Pinch the straight edges of each piece and attach to the left side of your purse as shown. Use a dab of water to secure it and press the top edge into the fondant.

5. Cut out a large daisy and attach it to the tails on your cake. Take a piece of fondant to make the center.

6. Paint the entire daisy and center with piping gel. Sprinkle white sugar crystals over it. Remove excess.

7. Make an opening into the top of the cake like the one in the picture. Make a small ring of fondant to go around the edge. Take another piece of fondant and roll into a rope 6" long and fold in half. Let dry. Stick down into the opening with a dab of water. Let dry.

YELLOW PURSE CAKE

You Will Need:

6" heart cake
3/4 cup yellow buttercream frosting
1-1/2 lbs. yellow fondant
Small Daisy Flower Cutter
Super White Luster Dust
Twizzler
Break a small white craft stick in half
Wax Paper

INSTRUCTIONS:

1. Cut an end off the side of your cake so that it can stand up on its side. Make two wax paper templates – one for the back of your cake and a strip for the top part of your cake.

2. Completely frost the cake with buttercream frosting. Place onto serving plate and refrigerate until set.

3. Roll out fondant. Use your templates to cut out the top strip and apply it to your cake. Now cut out the back piece and attach it to your cake. Run your finger along the edges to smooth it out.

4. Using your daisy cutter, keep cutting out small daisies to fill the front of your purse.

5. Roll a piece of fondant 6" long for the handle. Cover the Twizzler with the fondant. Insert craft stick into each end. Piece two places in the middle of the purse to make a hole and insert the handles down into the cake. Put paper towels in the middle to hold the handle in place until the fondant dries.

HOBO PURSE COOKIES

You will need:

Tear drop crinkle purse shaped sugar cookies
Tear drop crinkle cutters
Piping gel
Paint brush
4 oz. fondant in your favorite color
Specific tools listed below

INSTRUCTIONS:

1. Use your favorite sugar cookie recipe and the tear drop crinkle cookie cutter (second to the largest one in the set) to cut out the hobo purse cookies.

2. Bake on parchment lined cookie pans at 350 degrees until golden brown. Cool.

3. Follow design instructions below.

Mint Green – Roll out green fondant. Use tear drop cutter to cut out the fondant. Use the smallest tear drop cutter to cut out the handle as shown in the picture. Attach to cookie with piping gel. Use the Flower press from Wilton's Designer Pattern Press Set to make vine impressions on fondant. Cut out 2 calyxes and attach to purse.

Black – Roll out black fondant. Use tear drop cutter to cut out the fondant. Use the smallest tear drop cutter to cut out the handle as shown in the picture. Attach to cookie with piping gel. Use the large end of the large leaf cutter to make impressions on fondant.

Lavender – Roll out lavender fondant. Use tear drop cutter to cut out the fondant. Use the smallest tear drop cutter to cut out the handle as shown in the picture. Attach to cookie with piping gel. Use tip 81 to emboss pattern on fondant. Attach cut out to purse as shown in the picture. Imprint design around edge.

Pink – Roll out pink fondant. Use tear drop cutter to cut out the fondant. Use the smallest tear drop cutter to cut out the handle as shown in the picture. Use the Symmetrical Swirls press from Wilton's Designer Pattern Press Set to make 2 impressions on fondant. Cut out 2 large daisies and attach to purse with piping gel.

Chocolate Print – Roll out chocolate fondant. Use tear drop cutter to cut out the fondant. Use the smallest tear drop cutter to cut out the handle as shown in the picture. Attach to cookie with piping gel. Reattach the cut out with a little piping gel and fold over to the front. Use tip 2 at point.

Red – Roll out red fondant. Use Stampalicious cube lace to imprint fondant. Use tear drop cutter to cut out the fondant. Use the smallest tear drop cutter to cut out the handle as shown in the picture. Use the medium blossom cutter to make the center flower and 4 small blossoms and attach to purse – 2 on either side of the large blossom..

HANDBAG COOKIES

You will need:
Handbag shaped sugar cookies
2-piece purse cookie cutter
Piping gel
4 oz. fondant in your favorite color
Specific tools listed below

INSTRUCTIONS:

1. Use your favorite sugar cookie recipe and the small purse cookie cutter to cut out the cookies.

2. Bake on parchment lined cookie pans at 350 degrees until golden brown. Cool.

3. Follow design instructions below.

Yellow – Roll out yellow fondant. Use purse cookie cutter to cut out fondant. Remove excess fondant from strap area with the second cutter. Attach to cookie with piping gel. Use wavy cutter to cut horizontal and vertical lines as shown in the picture. Use small blossoms to cover each intersection and shoulder strap of the purse.

Red – Roll out red fondant. Use purse cookie cutter to cut out fondant. Remove excess fondant from strap area with the second cutter. Attach to cookie with piping gel. Cut two strips of fondant and attach to the cookie as shown in the picture. Use the stitching tool to make stitching lines down both sides of the strips. Cut out a fondant circle and use tip 3 to imprint the edges. Attach to the cookie.

Gold – Roll out gold fondant. Use purse cookie cutter to cut out fondant. Use tip 81 to make the design in the fondant across the bottom of the purse. Cut a piece of fondant as shown in the picture to go across the top part of the purse. Use tip 3 to make 2 circles in the top band and strap.

Aqua – Roll out aqua fondant. Use purse cookie cutter to cut out fondant. Remove excess fondant from strap area with the second cutter. Attach to cookie with piping gel. Use tip 353 to imprint design on purse. Add tip 3 accents as shown in the picture.

Green – Roll out green fondant. Use purse cookie cutter to cut out fondant. Attach to cookie with piping gel around the main purse area and carefully around the top strap area. Use the second cutter and an Exacto knife to remove the rounded part of the strap so that the top of the purse is intact. Gently fold the rounded fondant down over onto the purse as shown in the picture. Use a four-sided flower cutter to press into the fondant 3 times to make the design. I always center the first one and then add the other two on either side. Add green sugar pearls as shown in the picture.

Brown – Roll out brown fondant. Use purse cookie cutter to cut out fondant. Remove excess fondant from strap area with the second cutter. Attach to cookie with piping gel. Lift strap and twist. Use Wilton Decorating Comb (small teeth side) to press into fondant at an angle. Add small daisy flower and use closed tip 21 to emboss center.

Chapter 6
ACCESSORIES

Some women have tiaras... This cake is dedicated to them.

TIARA COOKIES

Be sure to make these for your Mom and anyone else you want to treat like a queen.

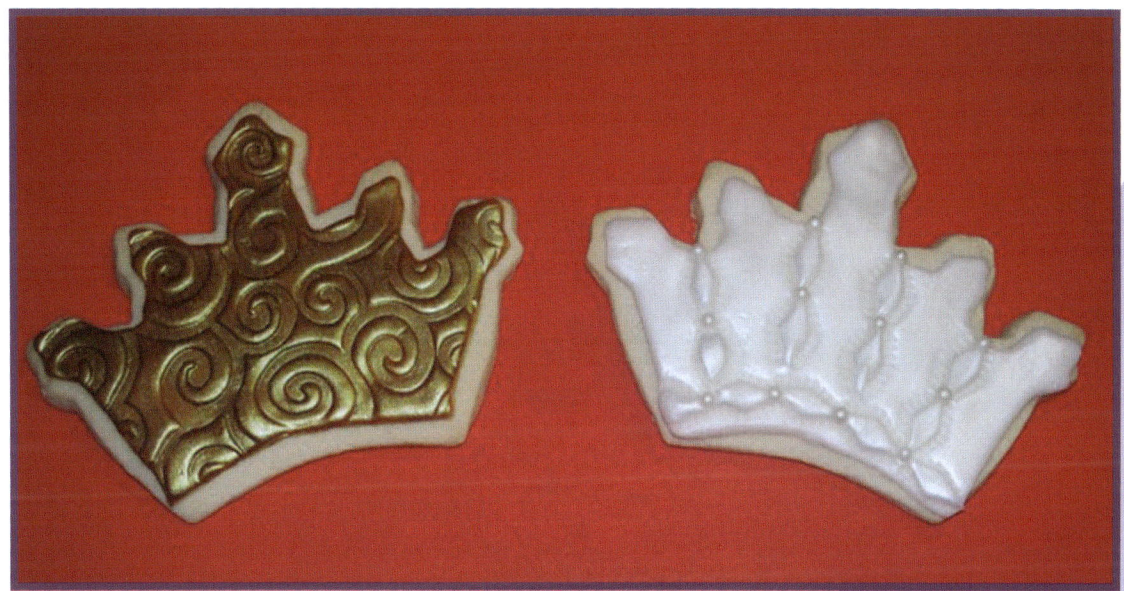

You will need:

Tiara shaped sugar cookies
Tiara cookie cutter
6 oz. fondant
Piping gel
Paint brush
Super Pearl Luster Dust

INSTRUCTIONS:

1. Use your favorite sugar cookie recipe and the tiara cookie cutter to cut out the cookies.

2. Bake on parchment lined cookie pans at 350 degrees until golden brown. Cool.

3. Follow design instructions below.

Gold – Roll out yellow fondant. Emboss fondant with Curlique rubber stamp. Cut out tiara using cutter making sure that a swirl is in the top center of the tiara. Attach to cookie with piping gel. Paint with Sunlit Cactus luster dust.

White – Roll out white fondant. Cut out tiara using cutter. Use crimper to emboss the crown as shown in the picture. Attach to cookie with piping gel. Take a dab of piping gel and use to attach ivory sugar pearls to crown.

DIAMOND RING COOKIES

I couldn't resist adding some "bling" to the book!

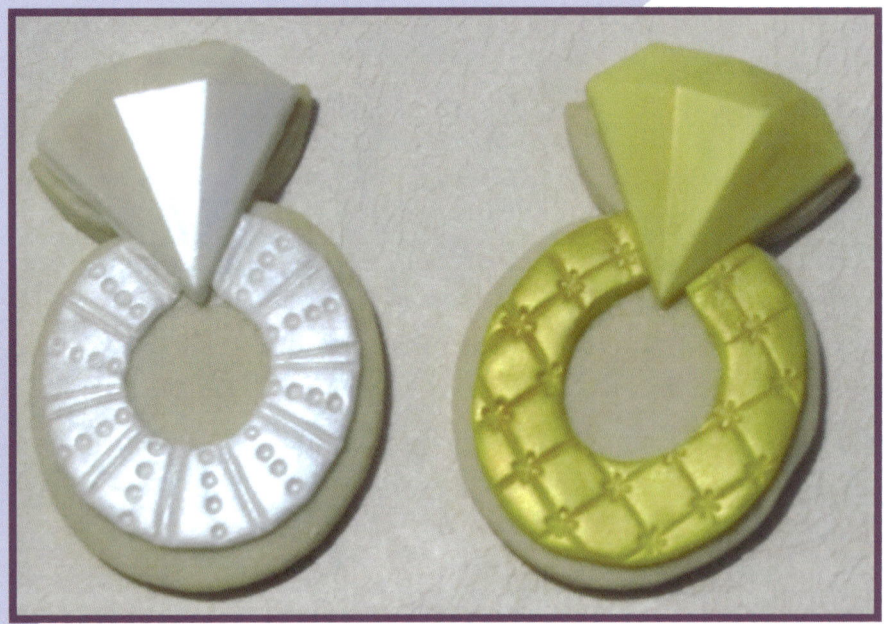

You will need:

Diamond Ring shaped cookie
8-10 Candy Melt wafers
3 oz. Fondant
Piping gel
Paint Brush
Luster Dust
Jewel Mold - use diamond shape

INSTRUCTIONS:

1. Use your favorite sugar cookie recipe and the diamond ring cookie cutter to cut out the cookies.

2. Bake on parchment lined cookie pans at 350 degrees until golden brown. Cool.

3. Melt your candy melt wafers and put into the jewel mold. Set in refrigerator for two hours to set.

4. Follow design instructions below.

White Diamond – Roll out white fondant. Cut out diamond ring band from the cookie cutter without the top part. Use 1" inch round cutter to create center of ring. Attach to cookie with piping gel. Make impressions around band as shown in the picture with a small pizza cutter and tip 3. Use jewel candy mold to make one white diamond with 8-10 white Candy Melts wafers. Use the extra melted chocolate to attach diamond to cookie. Dust top with Super Pearl Luster dust to make the diamond sparkle.

Yellow Diamond – Roll out yellow fondant. Use Quilting Patchwork cutter to imprint fondant. Cut out diamond ring band from the cookie cutter without the top part. Attach to cookie with piping gel just around the edges. Remove excess fondant from ring center band area with 2" inch round cutter. Use jewel candy mold to make one yellow diamond with 8-10 yellow Candy Melts wafers. Attach to diamond area of cookie with melted chocolate. Add diamond and dust top with Super Gold luster dust to make the diamond sparkle.

YELLOW BELT COOKIES

I love belts and hope you enjoy making these belts as much as I did.

You will need:

7 Oval shaped sugar cookies with holes pierced in each end before baking
1 lb yellow fondant
Black licorice strings or Ribbon
Piping gel
Wilton Designer Pattern Press Set, Corner Flourish press
Sunlit Cactus Luster Dust
Lemon extract
Paint brush

INSTRUCTIONS:

1. Use your favorite sugar cookie recipe and an oval cookie cutter to cut out 17 cookies.

2. Use tip 12 to cut out hole on each end of the cookie before baking.

3. Bake on parchment lined cookie pans at 350 degrees until golden brown. Cool.

4. Paint piping gel on cookies. Roll out yellow fondant and cut out oval shapes and add to cookies.

5. Use a pointed tool to come up through the hole on the cookie into the fondant and then use tip 12 to make the hole.

6. Use the Corner Flourish press to emboss the fondant as shown in the picture. Mix a little Sunlit Cactus luster dust with a little lemon extract to make a paint. Use this mixture to paint the cookies.

7. Cut pieces of licorice long enough to fit into the holes and go under the cookie. Make the end pieces longer to look like belt ties. (If using ribbon, weave ribbon through the back of each cookie so that the cookie stays together and only the top part of ribbon is shown.)

BLACK BELT COOKIES

You will need:

10 Square shaped sugar cookies with holes pierced in ends before baking with tip 12
1 lb black fondant
Paint brush
Piping gel
Black Non-Pareils
Quilting Patchwork Cutter
Black licorice strings or Ribbon
8 petal flower cutter
Gum paste tools
Glimmer of Gold Platnium Dust

INSTRUCTIONS:

1. Use your favorite sugar cookie recipe and a 2" x 2" square cookie cutter to cut out 10 cookies.

2. Use tip 12 to cut out a hole on the diagonal end of the square cookie sides before baking.

3. Bake on parchment lined cookie pans at 350 degrees until golden brown. Cool.

4. Paint piping gel on cookies. Roll out black fondant. Emboss fondant with quilting patchwork cutter and cut out 5 - 2" x 2" crinkle square shapes. Attach to cookies with piping gel on the center area only.

5. Roll out black fondant and cut out 5 – 2" x 2" crinkle edge square shapes. Attach to the rest of the cookies.

6. Use a pointed tool to come up through the hole on the cookie into the fondant and then use tip 12 to make the hole.

7. Cut out 5 black fondant 8 petal flowers and attach to the plain cookies.

8. Using the tip of a small rolling pin, indent the center of each 8 petal flower. Add piping gel to the center and sprinkle with black non-pareils. Let dry.

9. Cut pieces of licorice long enough to fit into the holes and go under the cookie. Make the end pieces longer to look like belt ties. (If using ribbon, weave ribbon through the back of each cookie so that the cookie stays together and only the top part of ribbon is shown.)

Chapter 7
WHAT'S IN YOUR CLOSET?
IMPORTANT TECHNIQUES

COLORING BUTTERCREAM OR FONDANT

Buttercream – The concentrated gel colors on the market enable you to add some of the most vibrant colors to your cakes. I use them exclusively now. The paste colors can get hard over time and glycerin is used to restore them. I've tried this but don't like the uneven color and streaks that end up in your buttercream or fondant.

Fondant – Pastel colors are easy to achieve in fondant. Just add a little gel color at a time. A toothpick is handy for this because you don't want to squirt a blob of color by mistake. Darker colors are easier to achieve if you buy them that way. In particular, I never make black fondant. It's easier for me to purchase it in 5 or 10 pound buckets.

TECHNIQUES

It is important to practice techniques before you make the actual cake or cookie. I do this by keeping fondant that has touched buttercream or piping gel in a plastic zip top bag. Just remove the buttercream from it and add confectioner's sugar or vegetable shortening to it to remove the stickiness of the piping gel and reuse it over and over again to practice various fondant techniques.

DOLL CAKES – Please do not be intimidated by the doll cakes in this book. They're very easy to make. Batter used for the fondant-covered doll cakes should be a pound cake consistency. If you want to use the lemon, chocolate or spice cake recipe in the back of the book, use a buttercream frosting design. I have covered these cakes with fondant before, and if you want to make the fondant designs with these soft crumb cakes, I recommend that you freeze the crumb coated cake to give it the firm crust you need to smooth the fondant. The mini doll cakes are great practice cakes to master before making one of the large doll cakes.

COVERING CAKES WITH FONDANT – Whenever you want to cover a cake with fondant, make sure that the cake has been covered with a thin layer of frosting and then refrigerated until that frosting has set. This is important so that the fondant can adhere to the frosting, and you have time to smooth it before the frosting comes to room temperature. If you cover a cake with fondant that hasn't been refrigerated, the fondant will be hard to smooth out, the frosting will probably ooze out of the middle and cause bulges in your fondant, and the cake will not look appealing. For examples of how to cover a cake in fondant, check out YouTube for videos.

COVERING COOKIES WITH FONDANT – I use fondant exclusively for covering my sugar cookies. After the sugar cookie has cooled, lightly paint it with piping gel. Cut out the fondant with the same cookie cutter, use a bench scraper to lift up the fondant cut-out and attach to the cookie. Let your fondant covered cookies set before stacking them in a box or using 4x6" poly bags to package them.

PAINTING WITH LUSTER OR PETAL DUST-- Luster dust and either a little vodka or lemon extract can be used to "paint" your fondant to give your design an overall sheen or highlight accents. I use palette trays for small jobs or bathroom cups to hold larger quantities. Some of the white luster dusts have different color undertones so be careful to label your palette trays or cups.

HOW TO USE TOOLS:

CRIMPER – Roll out your fondant 1/4 inch thick. If your crimper didn't come with a rubber band, place one around it and adjust it so that your crimper is as open as you want it. Play around with crimping your fondant at a 90-degree angle until you reach your desired pattern.

IMPRESSION MATS – Roll out your fondant 1/4 inch thick. Lay your impression mat on top of the fondant and then roll over it with even pressure. Use your bench scraper to lift the fondant off the mat so you don't stretch the fondant (or the design will be distorted). I look at the designs on the fondant and pick an area that shows off the pattern I want. For example, if you're cutting out a dress pattern, you don't want to put the cookie cutter through a flower unless you only want to show half of the flower on your dress.

PRESSES – Roll out your fondant 1/4 inch thick. With even pressure, put your press into the fondant and remove. You may have to practice this technique several times to get the right amount of pressure needed to imprint your design without messing up your fondant.

STENCILS – Roll out your fondant 1/4 inch think. Lay the stencil on top of the fondant and use your small rolling pin to roll over the stencil to secure it to the fondant. Put some petal or luster dust, cocoa powder, confectioner's sugar or cinnamon on a small plate with a piece of paper towel away from your powder. Using a paint brush, collect a little bit of the powder, and dab it on the paper towel to remove the excess. Rub the paint brush over the stencil lightly making sure that you stay on the stencil and rub in any excess as you go along. Once you make sure you've covered the entire stencil design, gently remove the stencil.

RUBBER STAMPS – Roll out your fondant 1/4 inch thick. With even pressure, put your stamp firmly into the fondant and remove. You may have to practice this technique several times to get the right amount of pressure needed to get the stamp to imprint the fondant in an even pattern.

TEMPLATES – I generally cut out two templates out of cake boards whenever I make them. I use one for the cookie dough, and one for the fondant.

STITCHING TOOL – This tool makes it look like there are seams in your fondant. Practice using it until you can get even pressure. I have also used rulers elevated over the fondant to make straight lines.

CANDY MOLDS – I love candy molds. If you've ever been in a cake decorating store, you've seen a huge variety of candy molds. You can use them for chocolate and fondant designs. Just be sure to let your chocolate completely set before removing it from the mold and always remove excess chocolate from the top before putting it in the refrigerator. I use my bench scraper for this. Always hand wash your mold and dry completely.

SILICONE MOLDS – Silicone molds make it very easy for you to make beautiful and intricate designs. You can make your own or buy them at cake decorating stores and on the Internet. They're very easy to use. You just add a mound of fondant to the mold and force the fondant down into the crevices and then release your design from the mold. I have also made chocolate designs with the candy melts with the same ease. Hand wash your mold when you're done.

FONDANT VS. CANDY CLAY

Fondant and candy clay make up a lot of the designs in this book, and I love both of them. Some people I know hated fondant before they tasted the fondant I use. I have tested various fondant products over the years and decided to use two exclusively in this book – Fondarific and Satin Ice. They gave me excellent results. I have made my own fondant in the past, and I like the recipe I've included in Chapter 12. It's a lot of work though, and since I prefer to bake and decorate, I leave the fondant making to the experts.

Satin Ice is a wonderful fondant that can be flavored with different flavoring. It's incredibly soft and feels like satin. LoRan oils are my favorite flavors to use with this fondant.

My all-time favorite fondant to use now is Fondarific because of the taste, ease of use, ease in coloring, and the fact that I can smooth it out and not have to worry about it looking like elephant's feet. I met Lois Judy and Laura Darnall on March 21, 2009 at the Capital Area Cake Show in Burke, Virginia. I was fascinated by the demonstration and walked away with a lot of Fondarific flavors. Needless to say, I've have been singing Fondarific's praises. Check out their website at www.fondarific.com and tell them I sent you.

Chapter 8
TOOLS AND EQUIPMENT

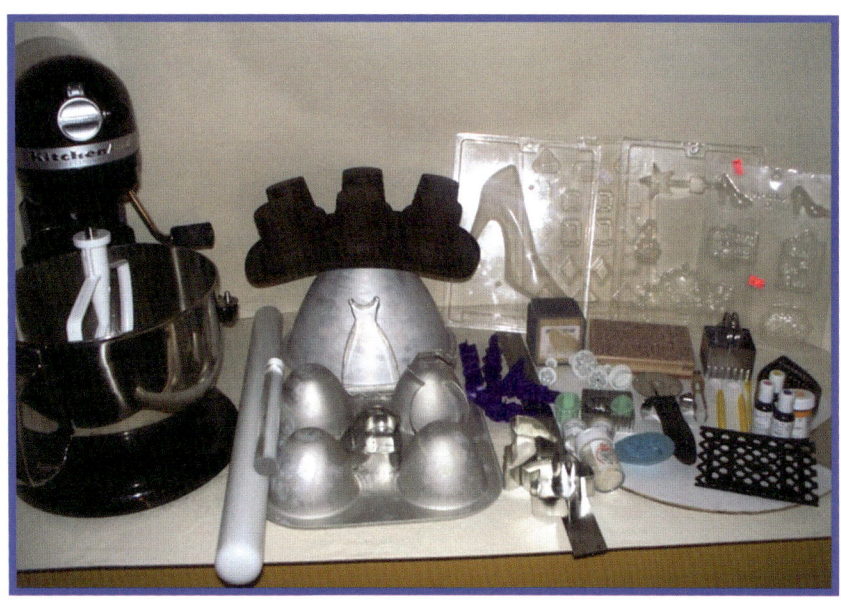

Here are pictures of some of the things I used to create the designs in this book:

1. KitchenAid mixer
2. Rolling pins in two different sizes
3. Wonder Mold cake pan
4. Mini Wonder Mold cake pan
5. Ice Cream cupcake pan
6. Wilton's Designer Pattern Press Set
7. Cookie cutters
8. Jewel Candy Mold
9. Stampalicious Cube
10. Shoe Candy Mold (1 section)
11. Various flower/leaf cutters
12. Rubber stamps
13. Icing colors
14. Edible glitter
15. Pizza Cutter
16. Petal & Metal dust colors
17. Silicone Mold Broach
18. Quilting Patchwork cutter
19. Stitching Tool
20. Square crinkle cutters
21. Ruler
22. Teardrop crinkle cutters
23. Yellow mistake remover tool

Not shown: Cake pans in various sizes, spatulas, toothpicks, paring knife, fondant smoothing tool, impression mat, wax paper, parchment paper, non-stick mat, cake boards in various sizes, foil to cover cake boards, cookie sheets, scotch tape, decorating bags, couplers and tips, edible sugar pearls, mixing bowls and lots of patience. ☺

Chapter 9
STORING AND TRANSPORTING YOUR CAKES AND COOKIES

STORAGE
CAKES

Buttercream - Cakes covered with buttercream should be stored in the refrigerator away from strong smelling odors. Make sure that you have enough room in the refrigerator. Please take into account the height of your finished doll cake, especially if you add a base cake. I have had to remove a rack in my refrigerator several times because I underestimated the height of a cake. Cakes should not be covered with plastic wrap in the refrigerator. It grabs the frosting and pulls it off when you move it. Cake boxes are better for storing your cake in the refrigerator.

Fondant - I have read over the years that fondant cannot be refrigerated. Both Satin Ice and Fondarific can be refrigerated with no problem.

COOKIES

When the fondant has set on your cookies, you can use cellophane bags to wrap them separately. This makes it easy to pass the eggs out or put them into baskets or give as gifts. I use tape to close them shaped to the cookie design.

I have shipped decorated sugar cookies all over the country even in the summer months with no problem. I use those decorated cardboard boxes you find at the craft stores. I line the boxes with waxed paper and fill them up with cookies. I fill in any spaces with bubble wrap, then wrap the entire box with bubble wrap and ship second day FedEx. They have all arrived with no breakage to very happy people who then shared them with others.

TRANSPORTING YOUR CAKES

Doll Cakes – I use a non-slip piece (comes on a roll, the same kind you use to line your cabinets) in the bottom of a large corrugated box with handles. This is so that when I put the cake in the car, it doesn't move. I recommend using a box that is larger than the base of your cake board so that you can easily put the cake in and take it out of the box. All of my cakes travel in the front passenger floor area. I know the cake won't move. There's nothing worse than spending time to make a beautiful cake and then having it arrive damaged. Last year I traveled to New York in late July with a car full of desserts for my Aunt Niecy's 70th birthday celebration. All of the desserts arrived in one piece, and only half of them made it to the party. The other half of the desserts, the caramel and mint chocolate covered pretzel sticks, and the chocolate mini bottles filled with liquors were devoured by my family.

Stacked Cakes – If you can, travel with the tiers separated and then assemble them when you get to the site. Otherwise, use plastic dowel rods. I like them because they're stronger, and you use less of them. I still use one or two wooden dowels to hammer down through the entire cake into the board so that the cake doesn't shift in transit.

A note on traveling with buttercream frosted cakes: Please make sure that your cake is chilled so that you can have a stress free trip. I remember years ago traveling with a buttercream covered doll cake over many speed bumps only to find that upon arrival at the party site that the cake has shifted and started to slide. I was very upset. Now I make sure that I have time to refrigerate these cakes.

Fondant cakes: If you use soft buttercream and cover with fondant without chilling the buttercream covered cake, you can have the same problem with the cake shifting during travel. I normally make my fondant cakes a day before I need them to allow time for the fondant to set before delivering them.

Chapter 10
GIFT AND PARTY IDEAS

GIFT IDEAS

All of the cakes, cookies and chocolate designs in this book make wonderful gifts. You can tailor the colors to your recipient's favorite color to make an even greater impact. I still remember the look on people's faces when I deliver cakes or cookie baskets in their favorite color or party theme.

Doll cakes – Make your doll cake covered in fondant. After fondant has set, sit the entire cake in an extra large plastic cellophane bag. Have a piece of ribbon handy so you can tie it closed over the doll's head and make a beautiful bow. The picture shows a doll cake and cookies that I gave to the First Lady of my former church for her birthday. She loved it.

Cookie Boxes/Baskets – Decorated cookies are a feast for the eyes so share them with special people. There are a variety of boxes on the market that you can use to fit any special occasion. Check out your local craft store.

Chocolate Shoes – Women love chocolate and shoes so this is a perfect combination. There are endless numbers of ways you can fill the chocolate mold and embellish the shoe. Your decorated shoe can be placed in a 2 lb. candy box with a clear top and wrapped with a bow.

DESSERT TABLES

Dessert tables are an increasingly popular sight at most parties and wedding receptions. I have done a lot of them over the years and have enjoyed the variety of things you can create with a theme in mind. My nephews have been some of my greatest testers, and I love to surprise them. For dessert tables, I include a centerpiece cake, several other decorated cakes, decorated cupcakes, decorated brownies, miniature cheesecakes, decorated marshmallow treats, handmade chocolates, caramel and mint chocolate covered pretzels, white and mint chocolate covered strawberries, and various candies or miniature chocolate bottles filled with liquor. The pretzels always disappear first.

When using various candies, remember to add scoops and decorative bags when you have candy containers filled with unpackaged candies so that people can help themselves.

Chapter 11
MY FAVORITE RECIPES

QUICK LEMON CAKE*

2 Duncan Hines® Lemon Cake mixes
2 cups water
1/3 cup melted unsalted butter
8 large eggs
1 small box Jell-O® lemon instant pudding
1 small box Jell-O® lemon cook 'n serve pudding
1 envelope Dream Whip®
2 tsp. Superior Lemon flavor (available at most cake decorating stores or
    online) – do not use lemon extract, it's too concentrated

Preheat oven and grease and flour your cake pans. Place all ingredients into a large bowl and mix until blended together for about 3-5 minutes. Bake in a 325 degree oven for cakes 10" or larger. Use 350 degrees for cakes 9" or smaller. Check on the cake after 30 minutes. The actual time depends on the size cake pan used. Makes (1) 12"x18"x2" sheet cake; (2) 9"x13"x2" rectangular cakes; (4) 8" or 9" round cake pans; (6) 6" round or heart cake pans; 24-36 cupcakes, depending on how much batter used.

Note: To be even more decadent, split each layer and fill with lemon pie filling to make everyone smile. For a lighter dessert, mix the lemon pie filling with an 8 oz. container of Cool Whip. For a special surprise when making cupcakes, spread lemon pie filling on the cupcakes before adding frosting.

QUICK CHOCOLATE CAKE*

2 Duncan Hines® Devil's Food Cake mixes
2-1/3 cups coffee
1 cup melted unsalted butter
8 large eggs
1 small box Jell-O® chocolate instant pudding
1 small box Jell-O® chocolate cook 'n serve pudding
1 envelope Dream Whip®
2 tbsp. Apple Cider vinegar
1 12 oz. bag of semisweet chips

Preheat oven and grease and flour your cake pans. Place all ingredients into a large bowl and mix until blended together on speed 3 for about 3-5 minutes. Bake in a 325 degree oven for cakes 10" or larger. Use 350 degrees for cakes 9" or smaller. Check on the cake after 30 minutes. The actual time depends on the size cake pan used. Makes (1) 12"x18"x2" sheet cake; (2) 9"x13"x2" rectangular cakes; (4) 8" or 9" round cake pans; (6) 6" round or heart cake pans; 24-36 cupcakes, depending on how much batter used.

Note: For chocolate lovers, split each layer and fill with chocolate ganache. Add ganache to the top of your cupcakes before your buttercream frosting, and you'll have everyone asking you for the recipe.

QUICK SPICE CAKE*

2 Duncan Hines® Spice Cake mixes
2 cups water
1/3 cup melted unsalted butter
8 large eggs
1 small box Jell-O® butterscotch instant pudding
1 small box Jell-O® butterscotch cook 'n serve pudding
1 envelope Dream Whip®
1 12 oz. butterscotch chips

Preheat oven and grease and flour your cake pans. Place all ingredients into a large bowl and mix until blended together on speed 3 for about 3-5 minutes. Bake in a 325 degree oven for cakes 10" or larger. Use 350 degrees for cakes 9" or smaller. Check on the cake after 30 minutes. The actual time depends on the size cake pan used. Makes (1) 12"x18"x2" sheet cake; (2) 9"x13"x2" rectangular cakes; (4) 8" or 9" round cake pans; (6) 6" round or heart cake pans; 24-36 cupcakes, depending on how much batter used.

*These recipes given to me by a wonderful woman named Margie, the former owner of the Little Bitts Cake Shop in Wheaton, Maryland.

CARROT CAKE

4 large eggs
1 cup sugar
1 cup light brown sugar
1 tsp salt
1 1/4 cups melted unsalted butter
2 1/2 tsp cinnamon
1 tsp pure vanilla
1/2 tsp freshly grated nutmeg
1 tsp baking soda
2 cups flour
2 cups grated carrots

Preheat oven to 350 degrees and grease and flour your cake pans. Combine all ingredients together in a large bowl. I usually hand mix everything together but you can use a mixer. Pour into two greased and floured 9" round cake pans and bake for 30 minutes. Let cakes cool in the pan for 10 minutes before removing to completely cool on a rack.

GLUTEN FREE CAKE MIXES/FROSTINGS

I'm still testing recipes for gluten free cakes. Right now I use Pamela's Products Chocolate Cake, Betty Crocker's Gluten Free Yellow Cake mix, Brownie Mix and Chocolate Cookie whenever I want something sweet. They also have gluten free frostings and other products. Check out www.julesglutenfree.com for gluten free flour that can be substituted in some recipes 1:1. Sign up for her newsletter.

SUGAR SYRUP

1 cup sugar
1 cup water

Combine sugar and water in a saucepan. Stir until sugar is completed dissolved in the water. Bring to a boil and then remove from heat. Let completely cool.

Variations: Add up to a 1/4 cup of the following: vanilla extract, almond extract, fresh lemon juice, fresh orange juice, strong brewed coffee. Brush over your cake layers and let cake absorb before applying the frosting.

BUTTERCREAM FROSTING

8 cups confectioner's sugar
1-1/4 cups powdered coffee creamer
1/2 tsp salt
1 cup unsalted butter, softened
1 cup Crisco®
3/4 - 1 cup liquid whipping cream
2 tsp vanilla extract
1/8 cup Creme Bouquet flavor
1 tsp dry van (availible in most cake decorating stores)

In a heavy duty mixer, combine together all of the dry ingredients. Blend together for 2 minutes. Add butter and Crisco. Mixture will be extremely thick at this point. Turn the mixture speed up to whip it a little more, then decrease the speed and add the vanilla extract and creme bouquet flavor. Start adding the whipping cream and beating well until you reach the consistency desired. I let the mixer blend this frosting for 5-10 minutes. The longer you let it blend, the fluffier it gets.

Variations:

Butterscotch frosting - melt 1 package of butterscotch chips, let cool until lukewarm and then add to frosting after the butter and Crisco has been added. Blend well.

Coconut frosting - substitute 1/2 cup coconut cream and 1/2 cup coconut milk, 1/4 cup whipping cream instead of the amount given for the whipping cream and use 2 tsp coconut flavor instead of the Creme Bouquet flavor.

Cream Cheese frosting - add 2-8 oz. packages of softened cream cheese when you add the butter and Crisco. Use 3/4 cup liquid whipping cream and add 1 Tbsp lemon juice instead of the Creme Bouquet flavor.

Grand Marnier® frosting - substitute 1/8 cup Grand Marnier® for the Creme Bouquet flavor.

White Chocolate frosting - add 1 pkg. melted white chocolate chips to the mixture with the butter and Crisco.

CHOCOLATE BUTTERCREAM FROSTING

8 cups confectioner's sugar
1-1/4 cups powdered coffee creamer
1 tsp salt
1 cup unsalted butter
1 cup Crisco®
3/4 cups unsweetened cocoa
1/2 – 3/4 cup liquid whipping cream
1 tbsp vanilla extract
3/4 tsp dry van (use another 1/2 tbsp vanilla if you don't have this)
1/8 cup boiling water
1/2 tbsp instant coffee granules

In a heavy duty mixer, combine together all of the dry ingredients. Blend together for 2 minutes. Add butter and Crisco. Mixture will be extremely thick at this point. Turn the mixture speed up to whip it a little more, then decrease the speed and add the vanilla extract and coffee granules mixed with the boiling water. Start adding the whipping cream and beating well until you reach the consistency desired. For lighter frosting, let blend for up to 10 minutes.

PEANUT BUTTER FROSTING

1-18 oz. jar creamy peanut butter
5 cups confectioner's sugar
¾ cup powdered coffee creamer
1/2 – 1 cup liquid whipping cream
2 tbsp vanilla extract
1 cup unsalted butter, softened

In a heavy duty mixer, blend together all dry ingredients for two minutes. Add whipping cream, extract and peanut butter. Add butter. Beat well until you reach the consistency desired.

CANDY CLAY

1-14 oz. bag Candy Clay Melts, any color
1/3 cup corn syrup

Gently melt entire bag of candy melts in a large bowl. Add corn syrup and quickly stir together to incorporate. Using cheesecloth or a lot of paper towels, squeeze the excess oil out of the candy clay mixture. This is hard work but gives you the best textured candy clay. Once you have squeezed out the oil, store the candy clay wrapped in two layers of plastic wrap and then put into a Ziploc bag with all of the air squeezed out of it. Let rest at room temperature for 24 hours. When you're ready to use it, knead it in your hands and roll it out like fondant.

CHOCOLATE GANACHE

1 (11.5 oz package) Ghirardelli® bittersweet chocolate chips, 70% cacao
1-1/3 cups whipping cream
1 tbsp vanilla or Grand Marnier® liqueur

Put chips in a large bowl; set aside. Heat whipping cream until it starts to boil. Remove from heat (or microwave) and pour over chips making sure all of the chips are completed covered. Let sit for a couple minutes. Add vanilla or liqueur. Using a whisk, beat the mixture until completely smooth. It is ready to be used on top of cakes. If you want to form it into truffles, put in the refrigerator until firm.

CUBAN OPERA CAKE

(A very special thank you to Sandra Mallut, Pastry Chef/Sales Consultant at Amoretti, Inc. for sharing this recipe. Check out their products at www.amoretti.com.)

4 ounces bittersweet (not unsweetened) or semisweet chocolate, chopped
  - good quality like Valrhona
2 cups all purpose flour
2 tsp baking soda
1/2 tsp salt - good french salt or kosher
2 cups (packed) golden brown sugar or dark mixture
1/2 cup (1 stick) unsalted butter, room temperature
3 1/2 tsp vanilla extract - Amoretti Crema di Vanilla #651 or #500 or
  #595 with specks 2 fold
4 large eggs
1 cup sour cream
1/2 cup crème de cacao
1/4 cup Amoretti Compound - Mocha Espresso #11
1 - 2 tbsp Cake Batter Compound Amoretti #3059

NOTE: Review when extracts/compounds are added, some flavors are added towards the end. Also with compounds you can go a bit towards taste, with extracts you have to be careful. They are very concentrated.

Preheat oven to 325°F. Butter two 9-inch diameter cake pans with 2-inch-high sides; line bottoms with parchment paper rounds. Dust pans with flour; tap out excess. Melt chocolate in top of double boiler over simmering water, stirring until melted and smooth. Remove from over water. Cool to lukewarm. Whisk flour, baking soda, and salt in medium bowl. Using electric mixer, beat sugar, butter, and vanilla and other compounds/extracts in large bowl to blend. Add eggs one at a time, beating well after each addition and stopping occasionally to scrape down sides of bowl. Gradually beat in lukewarm melted chocolate. Beat in dry ingredients in 3 additions alternately with sour cream (drain first to reduce water content) in 2 additions, beginning and ending with dry ingredients. Gradually beat in crème de cacao and mocha compound. Divide batter evenly between prepared pans; smooth tops. Taste batter and adjust accordingly to your flavor profile you are trying to reach. Spicy? Less Spicy? More Sweet?

Bake cakes until toothpick inserted into centers comes out clean -- about 35 minutes. Cool cakes in pans on racks 10 minutes. Invert cakes onto 9-inch cardboard rounds or removable tart pan bottoms; cool cakes completely on racks.

CHOCOLATE MOCHA SIMPLE SYRUP FOR CUBAN OPERA CAKE

1 cup water
1/2 cup sugar
2 tbsp Chocolate Mocha Amoretti compound #357

In a 2-qt. pot, add water and sugar. Dissolve sugar over low to medium heat. Once the sugar has been dissolved, lower the heat and add Chocolate Mocha compound. Taste and adjust compound addition accordingly. Let cool. Use pastry brush to brush on each cake layer as it is added to cake structure. Top side is sufficent. Poke some holes or run knife across in few spots in cake for better absorption. This simple syrup keeps cake moist and adds more flavor dimension.

BUTTERCREAM FOR CUBAN OPERA CAKE

8 oz. imported dark chocolate, chopped – good quality
1/2 cup sugar
4 large egg yolks
2 tbsp water
2 tbsp light corn syrup
3/4 cup (1-1/2 sticks) unsalted butter, room temperature
A bit of Amoretti Vanilla (see above options)
1 tsp cinnamon oil extract - Amoretti - powerful stuff #590 – to taste

NOTE: Not a bad idea to use Oil Soluble Extracts or Compounds when working with a high fat recipe.

Melt dark chocolate in top of double boiler over simmering water, stirring until smooth. Remove from over water. Whisk sugar, egg yolks, water, extracts/compounds and corn syrup in a medium metal bowl to blend. Add 1/4 cup of the butter. Set bowl over saucepan of simmering water; whisk constantly until mixture reaches 170°F – takes about 4 minutes. Remove bowl from over simmering water. Using electric mixer, beat until completely cool and thick – takes about 6 minutes. Gradually beat in the rest of the butter, a tablespoon at a time, fully incorporating each addition and stopping occasionally to scrape down sides of bowl. Beat in lukewarm melted chocolate.

MOCHA ESPRESSO MOUSSE FOR CUBAN OPERA CAKE

1/2 cup half and half
4 tbsp sugar
2 tbsp Amoretti Mocha Espresso Compound #11
4 large egg yolks
1 tsp unflavored gelatin softened in 1 tbsp water for 10 minutes
1 cup chilled liquid whipping cream - not half and half
1 tsp vanilla extract - Amoretti - see above options
1 tbsp Caramel Compound - Amoretti - to taste #318

Bring half and half, 2 tablespoons of the sugar, and Amoretti Compound to simmer in small saucepan over medium-high heat. Whisk egg yolks and remaining 2 tablespoons sugar in medium bowl to blend. Gradually whisk hot half and half mixture into yolk mixture. Return mixture to saucepan and stir constantly over medium heat until thermometer registers 160°F – takes about 2 minutes. Pour into a large bowl. Add softened gelatin and stir until dissolved. Using electric mixer, beat until cool – takes about 10 minutes. Using clean dry beaters, beat cream and vanilla and extracts/compounds in medium bowl until stiff peaks form. Fold whipped cream into coffee mixture.

Cut each cake layer horizontally in half and be sure to trim top make even and save scaps for use later see tip below. Place 1 cake layer in bottom of 9-inch-diameter spring form pan and with pastry brush cover entire cake with simple syrup and continue with each layer of cake. Cover with 3/4 cup butter cream. Place second cake layer atop butter cream; cover with mousse. Top with third cake layer. Refrigerate 1 hour to allow mousse to set. Spread 3/4 cup butter cream over third cake layer. Top with fourth cake layer (cake will rise above rim of pan). Cover and refrigerate at least 4 hours or overnight.

CHOCOLATE GLAZE FOR CUBAN OPERA CAKE

1-1/2 cups sugar
1 cup water
1/2 cup unsweetened cocoa powder
12 oz. bittersweet (not unsweetened) or semisweet chocolate, chopped -
  good quality like Guittard
1 pat of unsalted butter for texture/shine
1 tsp or to taste Cinnamon Oil Extract Amoretti #590
Decorate Cake with Edible Gold Dusted Cinnamon Sticks

Stir sugar and 1 cup water in medium saucepan over medium heat until sugar dissolves. Increase heat to high; bring to boil. Whisk in cocoa; remove from heat. Add chocolate; add butter, whisk until smooth. You can add a bit of Cinnamon Oil Extract if you really like it a bit spicy. Let stand until cool but still pourable, about 2 hours.

Run knife around pan sides to loosen cake. Release pan sides. Scrape excess mousse from sides of cake. Transfer cake on spring form pan bottom to rack set over baking sheet. Pour glaze over cake, allowing glaze to drip down edges onto baking sheet (use spatula to spread glaze over any uncovered spots). Refrigerate at least 2 hours to allow glaze to set. (Can be made 1 day ahead. Keep refrigerated. Let stand at room temperature 1 hour before serving.)

You can also decorate with Edible Gold Leaf. It looks amazing or Cinnamon Sticks powdered with Edible Gold Dust. Of course you can write L'Opera on top in fancy writing!

This cake you can replace the topping of Chocolate Glaze to the Chocolate Butter Cream and cover cake with fondant and decorations. The glaze would have too much moisture to add fondant too and the fondant would not stay on your cake.

Makes 12 servings.

SUGAR COOKIES

1 cup unsalted butter
1 cup sugar
2 large eggs
1 tsp vanilla extract
1/2 tsp lemon extract
1-1/4 tsp baking powder
1/4 tsp salt
3-1/2 cups all purpose flour

Preheat oven to 350 degrees. Cream butter and sugar together in a large bowl until light and fluffy. Add eggs, one at a time and then vanilla and lemon extracts. In another bowl, combine flour, salt and baking powder together, then add flour mixture to large bowl until completely combined. Do not over mix the dough. I usually roll the dough out immediately using various cookie cutters and place onto parchment paper-lined cookie sheets. I start the cookie sheets on the bottom rack of the oven and once the bottom of the cookies are set, I move the cookie sheet to the top rack.

CHOCOLATE SUGAR COOKIES

1 package Duncan Hines® Moist Deluxe Devil's Food Cake mix
1/2 cup melted butter
2 large eggs
3 tbsp liquid whipping cream
1 cup + 1 tbsp all purpose flour
1/3 cup Cappuccino mix
1 tbsp vanilla

Mix all ingredients together in a heavy duty mixer. Mixture will turn into a ball. Roll the dough out immediately between two layers of parchment paper using various cookie cutters and place onto parchment paper-lined cookie sheets. I start the cookie sheets on the bottom rack of the oven and once the bottom of the cookies are set, I move the cookie sheet to the top rack. This usually takes 5-7 minutes. Leave on the top rack for about 2-3 minutes until lightly browned. Makes about 14 medium sized cookies.

Bonus Recipes

FUDGE BROWNIES

1 pkg. Betty Crocker® Fudge Brownies mix
2 large eggs
2/3 cup melted butter
1/4 cup coffee or Cappuccino
1/2 tbsp coffee granules

Preheat oven to 350 degrees. Combine together all ingredients until blended. Pour into 13"x9"x2" pan that has been lined with parchment paper. Spread to edges of pan and make sure that it is smooth across the top. Bake for 20-30 minutes, depending on your oven. Cool completely in pan.

SUPREME BROWNIES

1 recipe brownies divided and baked in two 13"x9"x2" pans
1 recipe peanut butter frosting
1 jar Caramel ice cream topping or melted caramels
1-2 cups peanuts or 6-7 crushed Heath Bars

Take 1 layer of the brownies and place on a tray. Spread peanut butter frosting over the entire top of the brownies. Sprinkle either peanuts or crushed Heath bars across the top and then drizzle the caramel ice cream topping or melted caramels over the top. Place the second brownie layer on top and press down. Repeat the same procedure. Do not store in the refrigerator because of the caramel topping. Slice and serve. I've used mini loaf pan liners to set these in after they've been cut.

CARAMEL & CHOCOLATE DIPPED PRETZELS

1 container Caramel
  (found at most craft stores)
16 -20 pretzel rods
1 bag 14 oz. Candy Melts, Mint Chocolate

Make sure that you have a large enough work space to spread out your dipped pretzel rods before starting this recipe. Line your table with parchment paper that has been sprayed with butter spray. Melt caramel in microwave in 30 second intervals. It will be super hot so be careful. Dip your pretzel rods and remove excess caramel and place on your parchment paper. Let them completely cool. Lift them off the parchment and smooth the caramel that has settled on the bottom to fit around the pretzel. Be gentle or your pretzel rod will break, and you'll have to eat it. ☺ Melt your mint chocolate in the microwave in 30 second intervals in a deep microwave-safe container. Stir till smooth. Dip your caramel covered pretzels down into the chocolate to make sure you cover all of the caramel. Let the excess chocolate drip off (or tap the pretzel against the side of the container to make the excess chocolate come off faster. Put back on your parchment paper until set. Enjoy.

Chapter 12
SUPPLIERS/FAVORITE WEBSITES

Websites/Places to visit:

www.acmoore.com – Good place for finding all kinds of craft products.

www.allrecipes.com – Great for finding unusual recipes that have been tested by people like you who love to bake.

www.amoretti.com – This amazing company has 1,000 premium ingredients for all of your pastry needs. Also check out their Facebook fan page for the latest updates.

www.cakecentral.com – This is an incredible community of people who love cake decorating and share their pictures, recipes and tips. Check out the forums where you can ask questions and get great advice. Heath and Jackie do an incredible job with this site.

www.cookiecutterfactory.com – Cookie cutters in a variety of shapes that are reasonably priced.

www.earlenescakes.com – Check out Earlene Moore's website for the diamond mat as well as other great products, recipes, tips for cake shows/brides, and other information.

www.ebay.com – There are a lot of good stores and sellers on eBay. Do a search for silicone molds, cookie cutters and other cake/cookie/cupcake related products.

www.franscakeandcandy.com – If you're in the Washington, DC metropolitan area, stop by Fran's Cake and Candy Shop, 10927 Main Street, Fairfax, VA 22030. Phone number is 703-352-1471. Sally is absolutely wonderful to talk to and has a lot of products and gives tons of advice. Classes are given there and are listed on the website.

www.fondarific.com – Best fondant I have ever tasted, and it is gluten free!! Each color fondant is a different flavor. They have samples you can order. Say hello to Lois and Laura for me.

www.globalsugarart.com – My all-time favorite place when I am looking for foreign cake decorating supplies online. Alan and his crew have some of the most unusual products and magazines from different countries. Sign up for the monthly newsletter to get email updates with sales and new product information.

www.ices.org – ICES is an organization of people who LOVE cake decorating. They have an annual convention, a newsletter, recipes, and pictures on their website.

www.jenniferdontz.com – Check out her DVDs, chocolate shoe picture, crimpers and other products. Sign up for her newsletter.

www.julesglutenfree.com – Jules has gluten free flour that can be substituted in some recipes 1:1 and she gives classes. Sign up for her weekly newsletter. It contains recipes.

www.michaels.com – Has Wilton products in their stores if you don't want to order them. They also have a good selection of cellophane bags, beautiful paper, ribbon and boxes to make your baked goods look special.

www.pamelasproducts.com – Delicious gluten free products.

www.theboxdepot.com – This is where I get my cake circles and boxes.

www.whitestokes.com – White Stokes has the best piping gel I've ever tried.

www.wilton.com – Great for all kinds of products as well as information on cake decorating.

C

Cakes
  Blue & White Pants, 37
  Doll Cakes,
    Black, 4-5
    Gold, 10-11
    Grey, 6-7
    Wedgewood Blue, 8-9
    White Bridal, 2-3
  Green Pants, 36
  Mini Doll Cakes,
    Brown, 16
    Green, 15
    Purple, 14
    Red, 17
    Yellow, 13
  Leather Boot, 28
  Red Purse, 39
  Snow Boot, 27
  Transporting, 52
  Yellow Purse, 40
Chocolate Molds
  4" Shoe Mold, 22-24
  Jewel Mold, 27, 36
Chocolate Shoes
  Green, 22
  Pink, 23
  Red, 24
  White, 23
Cookies, Sugar
  Black Belt, 48
  Boot, 29
  Champagne Heart Dress, 19
  Diamond Ring, 46
  Dress, 20-21
  Handbags, 43-44
  Hobo Purses, 41-42
  Mini Hats, 32-35
  Pants, 38
  Purple Heart Dress, 18
  Shoe, 25-26
  Tiara, 45
  White Heart Dress, 19
  Yellow Belt, 47
Cupcakes
  Mini Hats, 30-31

D

Dessert Tables, 53
Doll Cakes,
  See Cakes, Doll Cakes

Dresses
  See Cakes, Doll Cakes
  See Cookies

F

Favorite Websites, 63
Fondant v. Candy Clay, 50

G

Gift & Party Ideas, 53
  Chocolate Shoes, 22-24, 53
  Cookie Boxes/Baskets, 53
  Doll Cakes, 2-17, 53

I

Impression Mats, 50
  Floral, 15
  Flower Fun, 21
  Paisley, 25-26, 38
  Wavy, 35

M

Mat,
  Diamond Impression, 29, 32
Mini Doll Cakes
  See Cakes, Mini Doll Cakes

P

Press, 50
  Animal, 25, 28, 32, 38, 41

R

Recipes, 54
  Buttercream Frosting, 56
  Buttercream for Cuban
    Opera Cake, 59
  Candy Clay, 57
  Caramel & Chocolate Dipped
    Pretzels, 62
  Carrot Cake, 55
  Chocolate Buttercream Frosting, 56
  Chocolate Ganache, 57
  Chocolate Mocha Simple Syrup for
    Cuban Opera
    Cake, 58
  Chocolate Sugar Cookies, 61
  Cuban Opera Cake, 58
  Fudge Brownies, 61
  Gluten Free Cake Mixes/
    Frostings, 55

Peanut Butter Frosting, 57
Quick Chocolate Cake, 54
Quick Lemon Cake, 54
Quick Spice Cake, 55
Sugar Cookies, 60
Sugar Syrup, 55
Supreme Brownies, 61
Rubber Stamps, 50
  Geometric Swirl, 13, 34
  Stampalicious Cube, 14, 20, 25, 41

S

Shoes,
  See Chocolate Shoes
  See Cookies, Sugar
**Storing & Transporting Your Cake
  and Cookies**, 52
Suppliers, 63

T

Techniques
  Coloring Buttercream or Fondant,
    49
Tools, 49
  Candy Molds, 50
  Crimper, 18, 49
  Designer Stencils, 25, 33, 50
  Impression mat, 29, 32, 50
  Silicone Mold, 35, 50
  Stitching tool, 20, 25, 50
  Templates, 50
  Wilton Designer Pattern Press Set,
    19, 29-31, 33, 38, 42
Tools and Equipment, 51

Debra J. Mosely comes from a creative family with talented hands. Relatives on both sides of the family are skilled at quilting, home decorating, cabinet making, carpentry, sewing and other crafts. Debra found her love in decorating cakes and has found many opportunities to hone her skills. Doll cakes have been her specialty for the past 25 years and beautifully decorated sugar cookies are her new passion. She has taken classes with Roland & Marsha Winbeckler and Colette Peters and has learned other techniques from numerous books, videos, cake shows and other decorators and cake designers. Debra currently lives in Sterling, VA, and can be contacted through AuthorHouse (www.thecakeandcookiecloset.com) to schedule classes and book signings.

Chapter 13
TEMPLATES

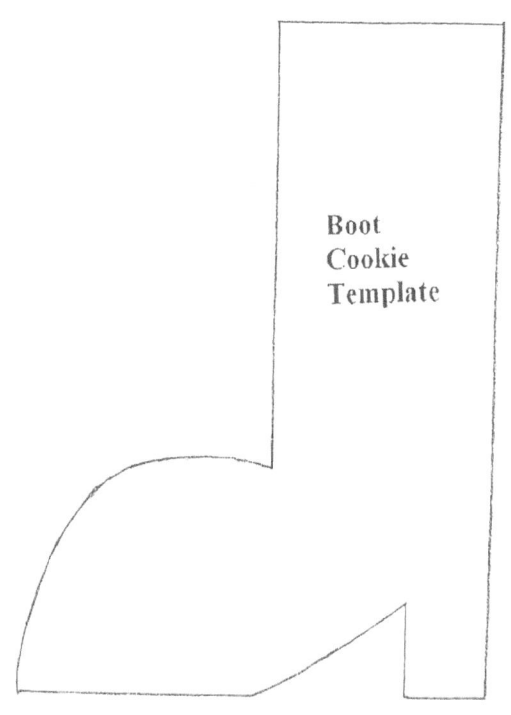

Boot
Cookie
Template

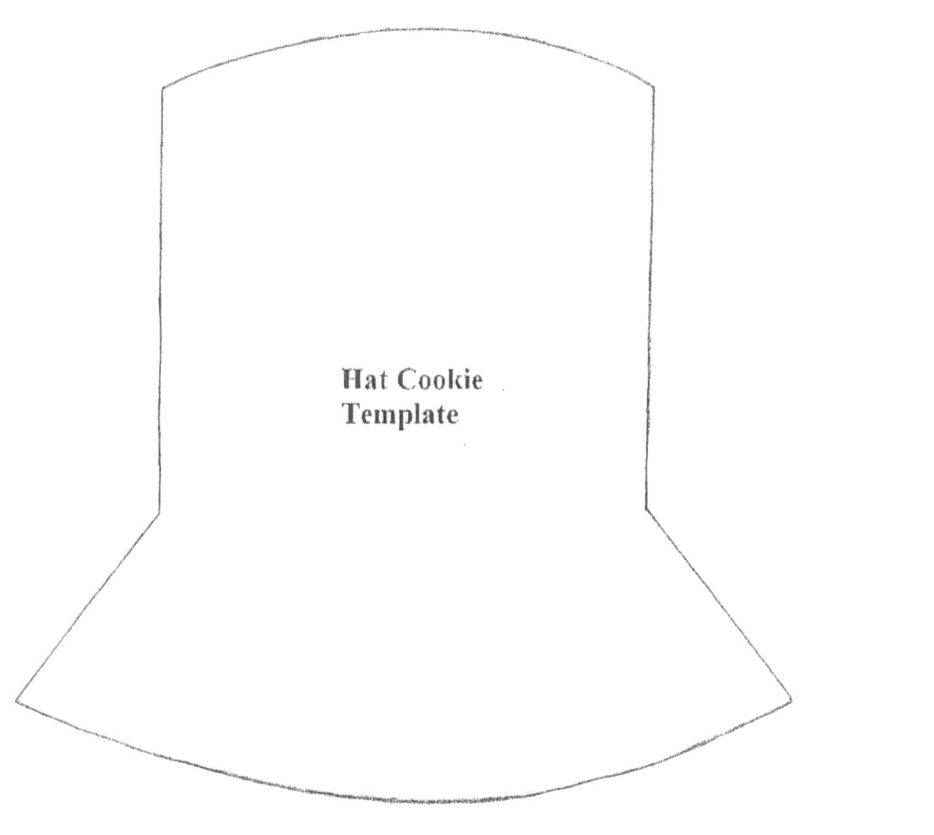

Hat Cookie
Template

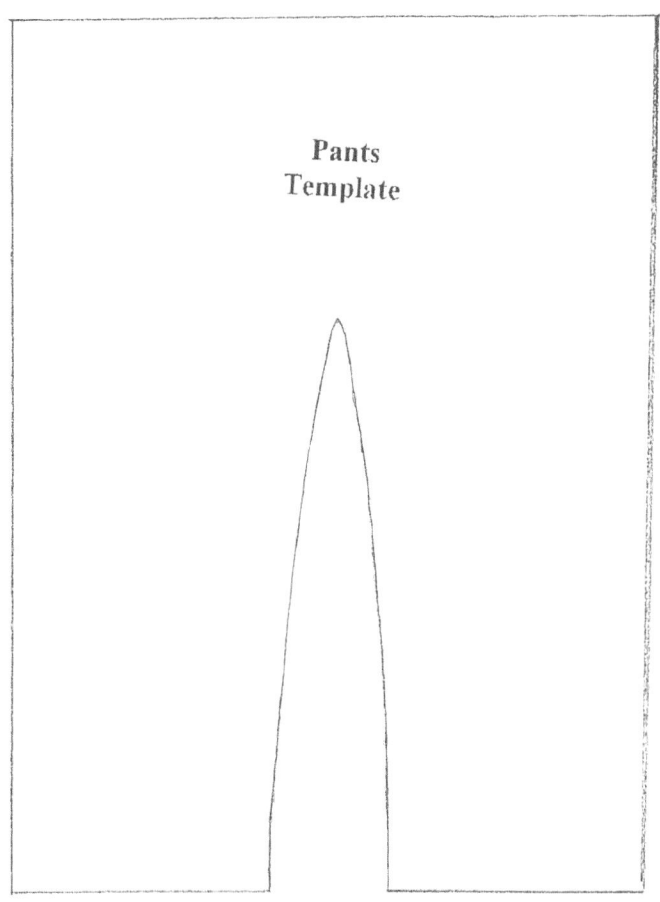

Pants
Template

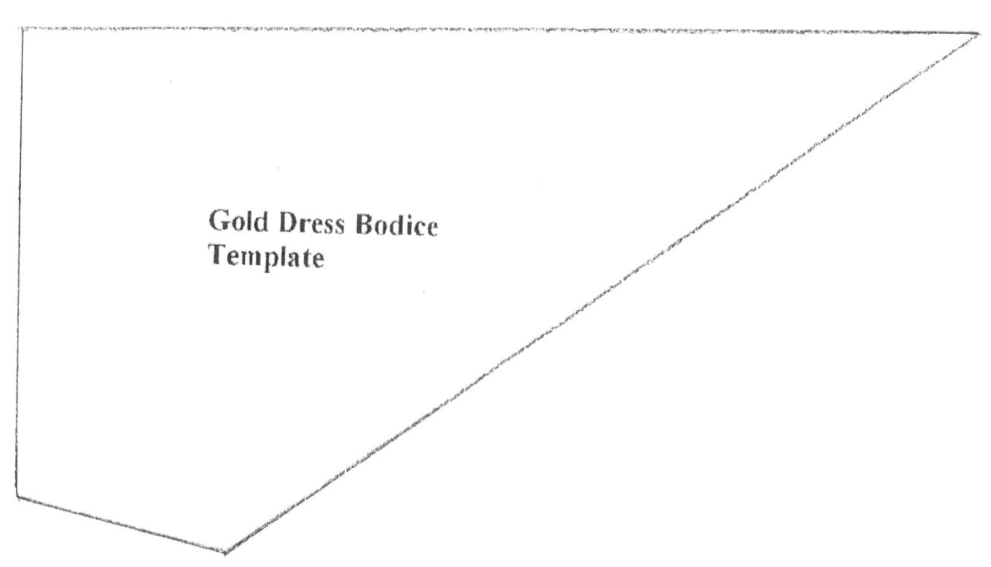

Gold Dress Bodice
Template

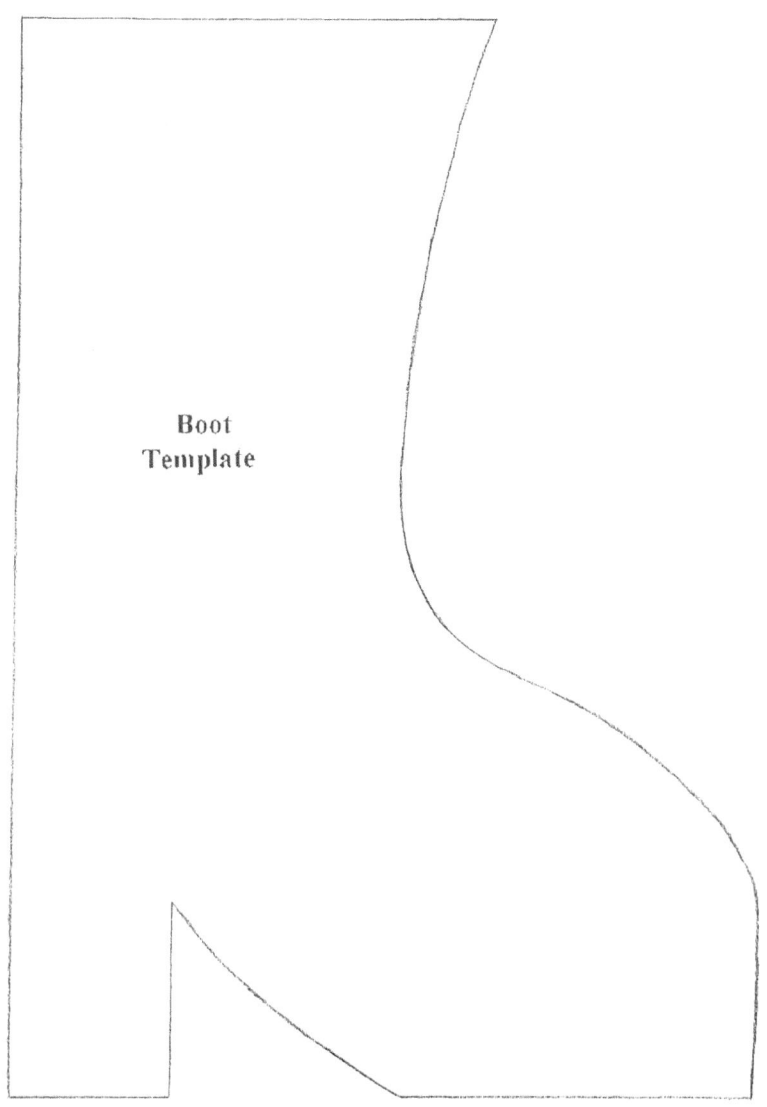

Boot
Template

9781438971339